TWENTIETH-CENTURY
FURNITURE

PHILIPPE GARNER

Phaidon

An Adkinson Parrish Book

Published by Phaidon Press Limited
Littlegate House, St Ebbe's Street, Oxford

First published 1980
ISBN 0 7148 2133 0

Designed and produced by Adkinson Parrish
Limited, London
Managing Editor Clare Howell
Art Editor Christopher White
Editorial Consultant Isabelle Anscombe

Phototypeset in the United Kingdom by
Servis Filmsetting Limited, Manchester
Colour illustrations originated in Italy by Starf
Photolitho SRL, Rome
Printed and bound in Italy by L.E.G.O., Vicenza

Contents

Introduction
Influences in Twentieth-century Furniture Design

Left Bentwood armchair designed by the firm of Thonet. This functional, elegant design adapted to mass-production is a classic, as popular today as it was when Thonet first introduced their bentwood furniture over a century ago.

Opposite Oak table designed by Charles Rennie Mackintosh; its simple, strong lines show Mackintosh to have been one of the first designers to have created furniture in the early twentieth century in a proto-Modernist style.

Furniture design has undergone more dramatic changes in the twentieth century than at any other time in its history. In a brief period of eighty years a truly Modern notion of furniture has evolved from the traditional attitudes prevalent at the turn of the century, when traditional concepts, which had survived effectively unchanged since the eighteenth century and earlier, still reigned supreme, even when disguised within the swirling lines of Art Nouveau or the exaggerated rectilinearity of the proto-Modernists.

Today, the very concept of traditional furniture forms have been questioned and in many cases rejected by the avant-garde. Hand craft and the machine have fought their battles and the machine has surely won, with craft being relegated to a still relevant but essentially anachronistic role. New approaches to domestic architecture and the trend towards built-in storage space have out-moded so many traditional forms of cabinet furniture. Meanwhile, the dramatic advances made in the development and exploitation of synthetic materials and the increasing sophistication of production techniques in the natural materials have led to the exploration of new forms for furniture. The two most important breakthroughs have been the exploration of new styles for series-production metal furniture at the Bauhaus in the twenties and the post-Second World War developments of synthetics, notably in the experiments of Charles Eames and the remarkable burst of manufacture of plastic furniture in Italy since the late sixties.

Introduction

The use of synthetic materials has been a notable feature of furniture in the post-Second World War period, often to create objects of considerable visual beauty. The table ('Stadio') and the chairs ('Selene'), designed by Vico Magistretti for Artemide in the late sixties, are as aesthetically satisfying as much traditionally crafted furniture.

The true phenomenon of twentieth-century furniture, however, is surely the development of the notion of Modernism, an ethic which gained tremendous momentum in the twenties and which still dominates in a variety of guises the approach of most leading international furniture designers. The twentieth century has witnessed the development of a conceptually new idea of modern furniture in which modernity has been expressed not merely by superficial stylistic changes, but by the fundamental questioning of old values and ideals and their replacement by new sets of rules, new ideas which have their origin in the Industrial Revolution.

The fundamental difference between the story of twentieth-century furniture and the history of furniture in other centuries is the shift in emphasis from the hand to the machine made. Today, the finest talents in furniture design are very often the industrial designers whose satisfaction is less in the handling and exploitation of fine traditional materials in an essentially élitist context, but rather in the solution of basic design problems with as wide a potential market in view as possible and with the realities of an industrialized society forming their guidelines. Design and industry have come together. We have reached a point of sophistication where, say, a chair, a single moulded unit of plastic, can be appreciated not just as the fruit of necessity but as an object of real beauty, the mechanical perfection of its machine finish accepted as every bit as aesthetically satisfying as the patinas achieved by the laborious hand polishing of wood furniture.

Introduction

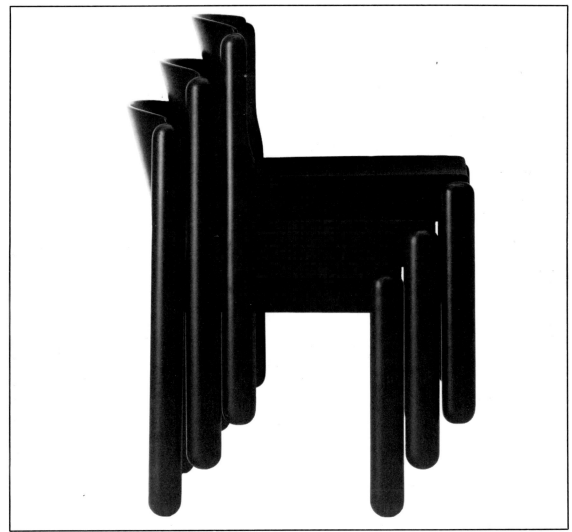

Left Stacking chairs made by one of the leading modern Italian furniture manufacturers, Cassina, have a sculptural quality which lifts them above the level of being purely utilitarian objects.

Below A growing regard for the practicality of furniture arrangement in the twentieth century has led to the development of such innovations as modular storage units and room dividers. The development of office and institutional furniture has been especially affected by the striving of designers and architects to find satisfactory solutions to the storage problems created by the modern work situation.

Introduction

The machine is the enemy neither of beauty nor of style. On the contrary it is the potential means of bringing both beauty and sound design to a vast public, if only that public, in turn, were educated to find a place for good design in its world. It is a great pity that in our consumer society there is no general education in design and it is a source of regret that manufacturers are all too often happy to cater, albeit profitably, to the worst instincts of an uneducated market. Despite the laudable work of so many pioneers, a glimpse at the stock of the average high street furniture shop the world over reveals the chasm that still exists between the tastes of the general public and the less-widely accepted creations of the perceptive designer and reveals the pervasiveness of mis-informed historicism and of downright Kitsch.

The concept of Modern furniture has a number of interesting precursors through the nineteenth century. These embrace the vociferous theorists and polemicists who exposed the problems that had beset furniture design with the advent of the Industrial Revolution and who sometimes made their own, not always rational attempts to solve these problems. They embrace equally the manufacturers who, whether by chance or design, found a successful formula for the mass-production of soundly designed furniture, and the few designers who sought and found a new stylistic purity. Notable amongst the former was the firm of Thonet, whose venture into the manufacture of bentwood furniture must be regarded as one of the great success stories of all time in the history of the furniture industry. Notable amongst the latter was

the British designer E.W. Godwin whose elegant ideas are regularly hailed as significant pioneers of modern design.

The history of the nineteenth century reform movement in design and industry has already been told too often and too thoroughly to need repeating in this context. Suffice it to say that from as early as the 1830s and 1840s attempts were made to resolve the conflicts of ideologies that had been brought about by industrial progress. A key event was the appointment in 1835 in Britain of a select committee 'to inquire into the best means of extending a knowledge of the arts and the principles of design among the people, . . .'

The Great Exhibition of 1851, conceived as a showcase for the industries of all nations and, undeniably, a magnificent occasion for the grand display of the wealth of achievement of the High Victorian age, served only to emphasize the dilemmas of the furniture industry. With all too few exceptions, the furniture on show displayed consummate craft and preoccupation with finish, but an excessive naturalism or eclectic historicism of style. Among the exceptions on exhibit in 1851 were designs from the Thonet factory, which were of unusual and unnecessary elaboration as well as the standard models which were at the basis of the firm's success. Another noteworthy exception was an exhibit of cast-iron furniture, including an elegant rocking chair, drawn in a simple curvilinear design which could hardly claim to be the earliest cast-iron furniture but which, in its functional simplicity and visual lightness, might be regarded as the precursor of Bauhaus innovations.

Below left and right One of the most important nineteenth-century precursors of Modernism was the English designer, E.W. Godwin, who was greatly influenced by Japanese design.

Opposite above and right below The furniture created by William Morris and his followers was an honest attempt to create a body of design in which suitability for purpose and respect for materials were of essential importance. Although these precepts were never put into practice with complete success in Arts and Crafts furniture, as in these cabinets (by J.P. Seddon, above, and Philip Webb, below) they were to become paramount considerations in the development of the Modernist ethic of the twentieth century.

Left A rocking chair of simple
curvilinear design, shown at
the Great Exhibition of 1851 in
London, but which could well
be seen as a precursor of
Bauhaus Modernism.

Introduction

Right and opposite above A regard for luxury and technical and stylistic virtuosity has continued to play a part in the development of the furniture of the twentieth century. The French Art Deco designers, especially, exploited to the full a vast range of exotic and expensive materials in their creation of fine and stylish furniture for a rich and exclusive clientèle. The screen (right) incorporates printed velvet designed by Emile-Jacques Ruhlmann, while the *chaise longue* (opposite), created for the famous apartment of Jacques Doucet, is in lacquer encrusted with mother-of-pearl (Legrain).

Below Alvar Aalto's own studio in Helsinki, showing furniture and interior design coming together in a fine example of Scandinavian Modernism.

The second half of the nineteenth century saw the gradual formulation of the theoretical background to the British Arts and Crafts Movement, with John Ruskin as a major influence and William Morris emerging as a key figure more for his reformist thinking and Utopian idealism than for his ability to find a truly satisfactory solution to the problems of furniture design in an increasingly industrialized age. The Arts and Crafts Movement in turn influenced the development of a more effective concept of Modernism, notably in Germany.

Amidst the eclecticism and stylistic confusion of the second half of the nineteenth century there came a salutary breath of air in the fashion, started in the sixties and developing through the seventies, for all things Japanese, and no furniture designer better captured the spirit of Japanese design than Godwin. He distinguished himself, especially, with a series of elegant ebonized wood cabinets, the stark, angular construction and decorative restraint of which mark them as significant precursors of the Modern Movement.

The story of the evolution of the Modern Movement is surely the strongest thread running through the story of twentieth-century furniture, with the development of concepts of functionalism and mechanized production as key themes. Fortunately, however, style for its own sake, humour, inventiveness and craft also have their significant parts to play. The story of furniture would be a dull and dry one if it were not for the regular displays of wit, style or technical virtuosity which have made the creations of the twentieth century so diversified and so fascinating.

Left A glass piano designed by Pierre Legrain in 1929; even within the essentially rectilinear approach of the first generations of Modernist furniture designers a certain element of the fantastic and surreal can sometimes be observed.

1900
Art Nouveau

Art Nouveau was a truly remarkable international stylistic manifestation, blossoming briefly and exotically around 1900 and just as rapidly fading from fashion. For the most part Art Nouveau became the victim of its own excesses and the fickle critics who had welcomed the novelty of its dominant curves soon advocated a return to a neo-classical simplicity of line.

The strongest international feature of Art Nouveau furniture was a return to nature as a source of inspiration, from the fully abstracted organic forms of certain designers to the richly symbolic naturalistic style of others. Whether abstract or naturalistic, however, Art Nouveau was essentially a decadent style and its overpowering character, so clearly shown in photographs of contemporary interiors, made it an all-demanding style in the domestic context. There is a certain aptness in the fact that the finest surviving Art Nouveau interior in everyday use is probably that of Maxim's restaurant in Paris, an exotic interior designed, appropriately, to be enjoyed for just a few hours at a time.

The organic Art Nouveau style found exponents, with distinctive national variations, most especially in France, in the twin centres of Paris and Nancy, in Belgium, in Germany and Austria, Italy and Spain. It was much less widely adopted as a style in the United States and Britain. The high point of Art Nouveau was the Paris Exposition Universelle of 1900, showcase for some of the most important exercises in the style, notably within the Pavillon de L'Art Nouveau exhibit of Samuel Bing.

Even in 1900, however, Art Nouveau had numerous critics. A British visitor, writing in *The Artist* on his impressions of 'Interiors and Furniture at the Paris Exhibition', was particularly scornful of the French contribution: 'In France', he wrote, 'modern furniture is unknown as yet... these rooms as well as those in the pavilion of "L'Art Nouveau" are filled with extremely costly furniture. The whole French section does not contain one good interior that would be accessible to the well-to-do middle class... Stimulating creations... can only be expected from France if architects and craftsmen will decide at last to consider the requirements of middle-class dwellings, and if citizens will desist from living their bourgeois life in surroundings that suggest kings and courtiers.' The same critic was full of praise, on the other hand, for the 'evolution towards the modern style, as has been clearly shown at this exhibition by England, Germany and Austria.'

It is more surprising to find the self-indulgent excesses of Art Nouveau being criticized by an artist strongly associated with the movement. Emile Gallé, writing in 1900 on his theories of furniture design, found fit to scorn '...the earthworms and tapeworms, the pseudo-seaweeds and frenzied noodles with which artists of undoubted talent thought fit, on the occasion of the 1900 exhibition, to make a cradle in which to shelter the twentieth century.'

There is a valid truth to such criticisms. French Art Nouveau was in many instances a pursuit of style for its own sake, an indulgence in the luxury of stylistic and craft virtuosity for a small circle of wealthy patrons. Few could afford the fine cabinet-making from Majorelle's workshops, the intricate carving of Guimard's fantasies or the rich silks and gilding of de Feure's precious furniture.

The path of progressive modern furniture has led, optimistically, towards the development of designs suitable for series production at widely accessible prices. A visitor to the French pavilions in 1900 could be forgiven for being unaware of this ideal and, in 1900, none could rival the French in their *forte*, the creation of luxurious and stylish furniture, a talent of which the international public was to be emphatically reminded once again a quarter-century later with the triumph of Art Deco in the decorative arts exhibition of 1925.

Right A bedroom suite by the decorating firm of Mercier Frères exhibited at the Salon du Mobilier of 1902. A commercial exploitation of the high Art Nouveau style, clearly demonstrating the overpowering character of this influential but short-lived fashion in interior decoration.

Below The Porte
Monumentale to the Paris
International Exhibition of
1900 where, among the many,
varied exhibits, could be seen
some of the finest examples of
furnishings and interiors
created in the Art Nouveau
style of design.

Paris **Bing/Colonna**

Samuel Bing was an intuitive entrepreneur and leader of taste. An early promoter of the arts of Japan in France, he became a shrewd promoter of contemporary design, both French and foreign, and in his Maison de L'Art Nouveau shop gave a name to the style which he helped define. Most able amongst the furniture designers whose talents he developed were Georges de Feure, Edward Colonna and Eugène Gaillard and it was these three who figured most prominently in Bing's pavilion for the 1900 exhibition.

Art Nouveau had its critics but many visited and were delighted by Bing's pavilion. It was easy to confuse novelty and modernity, especially when confronted with the seductive elegance of the suite of rooms presented by Bing. The wide pictorial coverage in contemporary journals and the ample surviving documentation makes possible a vivid recreation of these rooms which were the perfect expression of the Paris Art Nouveau style.

Gabriel Mourey, writing in *The Studio* of Bing's pavilion, described its situation in the '...left-hand part of the Esplanade des Invalides, in the midst of the Breton village,' and was impressed by '...the contrast between the calvaries, the granite churches, the ancient buildings and the modernity of this façade, adorned with a frieze of orchids in relief, and with its walls adorned by Georges de Feure's panels representing Architecture, Sculpture and Ceramics...'. Inside, the visitor could wander through a suite of passages and rooms which included most notably de Feure's Sitting Room and Dressing Room, Gaillard's Dining Room and Bedroom and Colonna's gracious Drawing Room.

Above An elegant carved wood table designed by Edward Colonna for Samuel Bing's Pavillon de l'Art Nouveau. A restrained example of Colonna's elegant Art Nouveau style.

Left A carved wood chair designed for Samuel Bing, *c*.1900.

Above Bedroom designed by
Eugène Gaillard for Samuel
Bing's Pavillon de l'Art
Nouveau. A perfect example of
Gaillard's Art Nouveau style
with its strong rhythmic play
of lines; even the grain pattern
of the wood panelling fits into
the patterns of flowing curves.

de Feure/Gaillard

De Feure was perhaps the most refined and versatile amongst Bing's protégés. A graphic artist of considerable sophistication, he evolved a distinctive personal version of Art Nouveau, refined, feminine and luxurious, and was equally at ease with a variety of materials, not least when designing furniture. His work has been described as a 'hymn to the beauty of women' and his interiors are exquisitely and seductively feminine. His predilection was for a pastel palette and he particularly favoured grey-greens and dusty pinks.

His furniture has been well described by Martin Battersby, a critic who has particularly appreciated the luxury aspects of French furniture and who wrote, 'De Feure's furniture was extremely graceful and elegant... (he) preferred gilding, which was a perfect foil for the delicate tints of the floral damasks and embroidered silks with which he covered his fragile chairs and settees. His rooms were reminiscent of Louis XV boudoirs in their frivolous femininity without the use of any eighteenth-century idioms of ornament. As an alternative to gilding, de Feure used pale woods but combined with unornamental panels veneered in a figured wood. . . .'

Eugène Gaillard's was an altogether more robust style, more emphatically organic, with full, sculpted frameworks and an obsessive cult of the whiplash line. In his Dining Room, Gaillard's table had a complex organic substructure which verged on the ponderous; the dining chairs were more successful with the sweeping lines of their framework and the tooled leather upholstery. The ensemble was dominated by a large vitrine-cabinet on which Gaillard's whiplash lines were allowed to run riot. In his Bedroom, Gaillard used a clever contrast of swollen organic frameworks of dark wood and panels of light wood in which the natural lines of the strong grain patterns became an integral part of the Art Nouveau play of line.

Below Dining room designed by Eugène Gaillard for Samuel Bing's Pavillon de l'Art Nouveau. Gaillard has brought together a variety of materials and skills in this definitive exercise in the Art Nouveau style – tooled leather panels and lush painted murals complete the rich character of this highly-decorated room.

Left Carved and gilt wood and embroidered silk canapé designed by Georges de Feure for Samuel Bing's Pavillon de l'Art Nouveau. Though the details are unmistakably Art Nouveau, the character of this canapé is strongly reminiscent of French eighteenth-century sofa designs.

Above Boudoir designed by Georges de Feure for Samuel Bing's Pavillon de l'Art Nouveau. Feminine, luxurious and refined, de Feure's designs make a contrast with the more dynamic lines and fulsome curves exploited by Gaillard.

Colonna/Charpentier

Colonna's was a more restrained style, closer to that of de Feure, and the furniture which he created for Bing explored the abstraction of plant forms in designs of disciplined silhouette. The centrepiece of his Drawing Room for 1900 was a vitrine of considerable refinement, its slender framework carved in orangewood.

The richness of these rooms was emphasized by the opulent wall decorations, by painted panels, embroidered hangings, velvets and lush floral patterns which pulled the schemes together, completing the concept of the total ensemble which was so much a part of Art Nouveau thinking in interior decoration.

Paris Art Nouveau found able exponents in the designers whose work was promoted by Julius Meier-Graefe through his La Maison Moderne gallery, opened in 1898. These included Abel Landry, head of Meier-Graefe's furniture *atelier* and two designers, Paul Follot and Maurice Dufrêne, who, after briefly exploring the vernacular of Art Nouveau, were to become leading figures in the transition towards Art Deco and in the popularization of Art Deco after the First World War.

Alexandre Charpentier, a member of the group 'les Six' formed in 1898, produced a limited number of furniture designs. The few known examples, however, including a dynamic music stand and cabinet now in the Musée des Arts Décoratifs in Paris, suggest a potential talent which regrettably was not systematically exploited.

Of all the Paris Art Nouveau furniture designers, architect Hector Guimard stands out as perhaps the most significant, if not the most influential. It was the style of Gaillard, with its more obvious elements – the whiplashes, the emphatic sculpted lines, the tooled leather and florid details, which was more easily copied by the Parisian plagiarists or by the provincial decorators who visited the Paris exhibition and went home to translate those features into the clichés of a provincial version of Art Nouveau. Guimard's mature style was subtle and his interplays of curves too elusive to be imitated. He became best known to the public as designer of the extraordinary cast-iron decorations of the 1900 Paris Métro entrances.

In his furniture designs Guimard evolved from an early exuberance to a mature refinement, a lightness emphasized by the choice of pale woods and carried through to the remarkable, confident delicacy of the carved details. One commentator, discussing a salon suite of 1907, wrote, 'At each natural join or ending Guimard has created exquisite and unique carvings, based on natural forms and movements evolved into abstract patternings and ripples; recalling, for instance, da Vinci's famous drawings of flowing water.' Guimard's style was the product of an intellectual commitment to the organic concept of environment and he pursued his version of Art Nouveau for some years after the style had been ousted from fashion-conscious circles.

Right Music cabinet in carved sycamore designed by Alexandre Charpentier, 1900. This strongly sculptural piece of furniture was exhibited at the Salon of 1901. The bronze panels sculpted in low relief on symbolic themes reflect Charpentier's versatility. He distinguished himself as a medallist and worked in a wide variety of materials.

Opposite A remarkable cabinet in carved pearwood designed by Hector Guimard, *c*.1900. The deliberate and emphatic asymmetry, the elegant sweeping buttress and the subtle abstract organic carving of details are the distinctive features of Guimard's personal version of Art Nouveau.

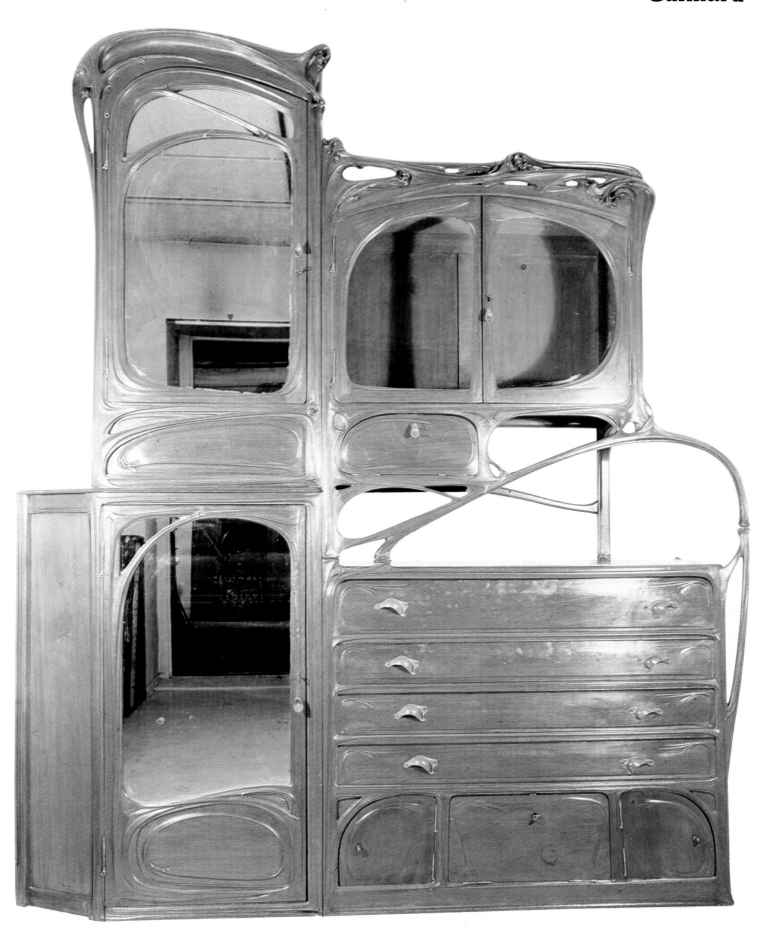

Nancy Gallé

Below right Detail of marquetry and carved glass decoration conceived by Emile Gallé for the spectacular bed *Aube et Crépuscule*, designed in 1904, the last year of Gallé's life. Inlaid in a rich variety of fruitwoods and exotic woods in their natural colours and mother-of-pearl, the marquetry work is remarkable for being sculpted in low relief.

Opposite below left *La Forêt Lorraine*, a carved wood desk designed by Emile Gallé and shown at the Paris International Exhibition of 1900. Essentially conservative in form, this desk is nonetheless fascinating in the details of the naturalistic structure and marquetry decoration. The title refers to the symbolic theme on which the decoration is based and is taken from the line of verse by Baudelaire inlaid in marquetry.

After 1900 Art Nouveau continued to flourish more vigorously in the provinces than in Paris, where the great exhibition of that year marked both the high point and the *aboutissement* of the style. In the more prosperous provincial cities Art Nouveau rooms were regarded as status symbols amongst the bourgeoisie until about 1905 or even as late as 1910.

The personal vision of one artist, however, had made one provincial town, Nancy, a centre of creativity in furniture production to rival the former autonomy of Paris. Emile Gallé, though primarily concerned with the techniques of glass-making, became interested in furniture during the 1880s, presented his first exhibit in 1889 and, by 1900, had evolved a naturalistic version of Art Nouveau and had inspired a group of local cabinet-makers to follow his principles of furniture design. The hallmarks of Gallé's own furniture were the logical derivation of all structural elements from specific plant, or occasionally animal, themes; the

application of Japanese notions of stylization; the use of the natural colours of a wide range of fruitwoods and exotic imported woods; and the extensive use of marquetry decoration.

Gallé was very much responsible for the revival of marquetry and, eschewing the tightly disciplined patterns of traditional marquetry decoration, he developed a distinctive pictorial style which exploited the colours and grain-patterns of a wide variety of woods. Floral and insect subjects were the most popular themes in his marquetry, but the range included animal, figure and landscape subjects. To the known techniques of flat marquetry, Gallé added personal variations which included the carving of certain details in low relief, the application of carved glass insects and the decorative use of inlaid mother-of-pearl. The magnificent bed, *Aube et Crépuscule*, made in the last year of his life, 1904, is a fitting *finale*, a *tour de force* of marquetry work and, in its concept, laden with richly poetic symbolism.

Above Carved wood stand 'aux feuilles de bananier' designed by Emile Gallé, *c.*1900. A characteristic and elegant example of Gallé's idea of creating a piece of furniture on a specific theme inspired from nature. Gallé was strongly committed to the ideal of deriving forms for structure and decoration from natural plant, floral or insect forms.

Gallé

Left Marquetry table top, detail of a two-tiered table from the Gallé workshops. Gallé made a speciality of marquetry and encouraged a revival of marquetry decoration. This table top ably demonstrates his skill in selecting woods with appropriate grain pattern and colour within the overall pictorial composition.

Below Display cabinet from the workshops of Emile Gallé, carved wood and marquetry decoration. In studying the furniture from a large workshop such as that run by Emile Gallé, it must be remembered that, although he was the inspiration behind the distinctive look of all the furniture, not every piece was designed by him and there were inevitably several levels of quality, from spectacular exhibition pieces to modest commercial designs.

Majorelle

Below Longcase clock designed by Louis Majorelle in carved woods with marquetry decoration, *c*.1900.

Below right Armchair in carved oak designed by Louis Majorelle, *c*.1900. Majorelle was the most talented of the Nancy designers to come under Gallé's influence. Although many of his designs are in a naturalistic style inspired by Gallé, at his best Majorelle worked in a strong, abstract, sculptural style.

In 1901 Gallé founded the Ecole de Nancy, a grouping of the artists and craftsmen who had come under the influence of his design theories. Most prominent amongst the furniture makers of this provincial alliance was Louis Majorelle, inheritor of a family cabinet-making firm and, until his encounters with Gallé, involved in non-creative reproduction work. Swept along with Gallé's enthusiasm for the naturalistic style, Louis Majorelle evolved as a leading figure in French Art Nouveau and became, for many critics, the foremost cabinet-maker in the style, at his best carrying forward the eighteenth-century traditions of French furniture. If Ruhlmann is to be regarded as the twentieth-century Riesener, then Majorelle is, surely, the direct descendant of the great *ébénistes* of the Louis XV era.

Majorelle, a gentle-looking figure with a pointed beard and an eccentric fondness for North-African dress, built up a highly successful business, with outlets in Paris, Lyon and Lille before retiring to North Africa. Much of his production was a commercial version of the Gallé style, though he showed himself adept in the exploitation of marquetry decoration and naturalistic carving. Majorelle's reputation, however, rests above all on his development of a personal abstract organic style, incorporating full, fluid forms carved in rich mahogany, counter-pointed with stylized plant motifs in the gilt-bronze mounts which tie these creations to eighteenth-century traditions. He designed suites for bedroom, salon or study with gilt-bronze mounts on such themes as the orchid and the lily. Perhaps his most spectacular creation was the bed 'aux nénuphars' of which two examples are so far known, one made for the Emperor of Germany's Strasburg palace. The gilt-bronze details of the bed are integrated with a fluid smoothness into the sensual, melting forms of the sculpted mahogany.

Amongst the other notable furniture designers in the Ecole de Nancy group were Eugène Vallin and Jacques Gruber, both of whom explored organic sculpted forms with a tendency towards an overbearing provincial ponderousness. In the Musée de L'Ecole de Nancy is a remarkable dining room by Vallin which clearly demonstrates the dangers of applying this heavy organic style, over-charged with naturalistic details, to the creation of a complete room.

Right Desk and Chair 'aux orchidées' designed by Louis Majorelle, carved mahogany and gilt bronze, *c*.1905; Majorelle at his best, using quality materials in a virile, sculptural expression of Art Nouveau.

Top *Sellette* in carved oak, attributed to Eugène Vallin, a member of the Ecole de Nancy. A gracious example of the abstract organic style, the curves of this piece flow effortlessly in unbroken lines, *c.*1900.

Above Carved wood bed, attributed to Eugène Vallin, *c.*1900. The heavy sculptural forms of this bed are typical of the work of Vallin and of the few Nancy designers who made the progression from the naturalism preached by Gallé to an abstract interpretation of natural forms.

Above Buffet in carved oak with panels of cameo glass, designed by Jacques Gruber in 1904. A piece of cabinet-making of undoubted quality, the proportions of this piece are, however, ponderous and provincial in character.

Belgium Van de Velde

The idea of total organic environment in the Art Nouveau style found considerable favour in Belgium, in the work of a group of architects and designers who came together in the 1890s as the Libre Esthétique group. The most prominent figures in this revitalization of Belgian design were the architects Henry Van de Velde and Victor Horta, both of whom developed strong Art Nouveau styles involving the dynamic play of line. Van de Velde's influence was far-reaching and by the turn of the century he had become a truly international figure, designing in Paris for Samuel Bing, creating the façade and fittings for La Maison Moderne, working in Berlin, and settling finally in Weimar where, in 1906, he supervised the foundation of the Kunstgewerbeschule, forerunner of the Bauhaus. In his interior schemes Van de Velde's essentially plain furniture became just one element in the harmonious mix of Art Nouveau motifs on carpets, stencilled wall decorations, carved *boiseries*, windows, even the Art Nouveau dresses designed to be worn in his interiors. In isolation many of his furniture designs somehow appear to lack the credibility and character which they assume within the master plans.

The same might be said of Horta's furniture designs, though as an interior architect he was brilliant, fusing such a variety of materials, cast iron, stained glass, sculpted wood, tiles and bronze in schemes of an extraordinary airiness and elegance, pulled together by his restless, playful *leitmotif*, the whiplash line.

Another member of the Libre Esthétique group, Gustave Serrurier-Bovy, became the foremost commercial designer and manufacturer of Belgian Art Nouveau-style furniture, characterized by the distinctively Belgian interplay of strong abstract lines. In 1899 he set up a factory in Liège.

Right Interior and furnishings designed for La Maison Moderne, Paris, in 1898 by Henry Van de Velde. Van de Velde was a major figure in the evolution of thinking from Art Nouveau through to a more truly modern style and his work was seldom as indulgent as that of his French, or even certain Belgian contemporaries.

Below left A selection of chairs designed by Henry Van de Velde in 1895 for his home, Bloemenwerf.

Below right Cabinet designed by Henry Van de Velde, oak, c.1895.

Opposite top left Cabinet designed by Henry Van de Velde in 1895 for his home, Bloemenwerf. Of simple and logical construction, this design shows Van de Velde's natural instincts as a precursor of Modernism rather than a decorative stylist.

Opposite top right and bottom left Two interior views of architectural and decorative schemes by Victor Horta, for whom the structure and the furnishings of a building were inseparable elements. Carved wood, stained glass, tiling, bronze and iron work combine in schemes of a satisfying organic unity. The interiors are of Horta's own home, undertaken in 1898 and now preserved as a museum.

Above Furniture designed
and manufactured by Gustave
Serrurier-Bovy, *c.*1900.
This designer was the major
commercial manufacturer of
Belgian Art Nouveau
furniture.

Germany/Austria

Below Furniture by Peter Behrens. Behrens, like Van de Velde, was a committed pioneer of the Modern Movement, but like so many designers at the turn of the century, he was briefly attracted by the Art Nouveau style, though never in an indulgently or flamboyantly decorative manner.

Below top right Wash stand by August Endell, *c*.1900.

Below bottom right Carved wood piano by the Balwin Piano Co., Cincinnati. Exhibited at the Paris International Exhibition of 1900, this is an unusually lush example of American Art Nouveau, using naturalistic motifs and a carved figure.

Opposite top Room setting designed by Bernhard Pankok, Paris, 1900.

In Germany and Austria the exuberant curvilinear styles associated with French and Belgian Art Nouveau furniture found less favour than the more rational rectilinear styles with which Austrian and German designers were to lead the way as the true pioneers of modern furniture design. In Austria in particular, and especially after the fruitful exchange of ideas with Charles Rennie Mackintosh, the straight line ruled supreme in the early years of the twentieth century.

In Germany, however, curvilinear Art Nouveau found a market at the popular level in the production of such manufacturers as Möbel Fabrik Olbernau, and also found favour with a number of designers, notably the Munich group, which included August Endell, Hermann Obrist, Bernhard Pankok and Richard Riemerschmid. For a brief period around 1900 they explored the language of organic Art Nouveau, Endell and Obrist producing furniture with curiously anthropomorphic details reminiscent of bone joints. Riemerschmid was responsible for a particularly pleasing chair design in dark-stained oak with sweeping sides flowing into the front legs and back support.

Van de Velde, who had moved to Berlin in 1899, furnished and fitted at least two interiors there the following year in his high Art Nouveau style, the Haby Barbershop and the Havana Company Cigar Store in the Mohrenstrasse. The latter was a particularly successful, though extravagantly non-functional exercise in the decorative curvilinear Art Nouveau style, the rhythmic linear theme carried through from seat, counter and cabinet furniture to the integral wood fittings and friezes. Of the avant-garde Austrian group, Joseph Olbrich showed most affinity with the curvilinear school of design for a brief period around 1900.

In England and the United States, as in Germany and Austria, the fluid high Art Nouveau mode enjoyed favour only in isolated instances, never becoming a major feature of national design trends. There are, however, a few good examples of curvilinear American Art Nouveau. Perhaps the most oft-quoted example is Charles Rohlfs' chair of *c*. 1898. But despite the frenzied interplay of lines in the high back carved by George Thiele, the structure of the chair is rigidly rectangular and the back two-dimensional. A more worthy example would be the naturalistically carved piano by the Balwin Piano Company, Cincinnati, included in the Paris exhibition of 1900. The frame is carved to resemble tree trunks, the stylized branches meeting in the centre above a high-relief carved figure of an Art Nouveau draped maiden.

In England many furniture makers made half-hearted compromises with the curvilinear style, though generally restricting its application to marquetry inlays. The English were more at ease with the 'honest' cosy comfort of rustic oak and celtic ornamentation.

Above Interior presented by
Joseph Olbrich at the Paris
International Exhibition of
1900. An unusually curvilinear
decorative scheme from a
designer who was a major
pioneer of Modernism.

Above Interior of the Havana
Co. Cigar Store, Berlin,
designed by Henry Van de
Velde in 1900. A strong, unified
scheme in Van de Velde's
distinctive style and doubtless
commercially successful.

Spain/Italy

The story of Art Nouveau furniture would be incomplete if it did not include the work of two remarkable, isolated talents: architect-designer Antonio Gaudí in Barcelona and Carlo Bugatti of Milan.

In Italy, a number of cabinet-makers indulged in a florid and baroque, though largely undistinguished version of Art Nouveau. Bugatti was an eccentric exception. Having evolved a highly personal style of furniture during the 1880s and 1890s in pseudo-arab taste and incorporating painted vellum, wrought brass or copper and inlaid woods, he surprised his public with his quite extraordinary suite of rooms created for the Turin International Exhibition of 1902, in which he integrated the organic concept with his own distinctive use of materials and decorative details. For these rooms he created furniture with sweeping lines, the wooden structure completely disguised by a covering of painted vellum; sweeping serpentine banquettes incorporating cabinets; and chairs drawn in unbroken lines. A bewildered jury was unanimous in awarding him the Prix d'Honneur.

In Barcelona, Antonio Gaudí, the baroque genius of Art Nouveau architecture, designed inventive furniture to complement his organic architecture. His distinctive style had something of the knobbly-joint look of the Munich group's furniture. Among his more interesting experiments was the combined use of carved wood and wrought iron, as in his pews for the chapel of the Colonia Güell.

Art Nouveau found able exponents in the field of furniture design, many of them architects committed to the ideal of total organic environments. The over-indulgences of the style, however, were short-lived, as fashion demanded changes and the evolution of thinking toward a truly modern style of furniture design scorned the decadent excesses of this decorative mode.

Right and below A variety of designs for seat furniture by Spanish architect Antonio Gaudí, *c.*1900. Best known as an architect, Gaudí, however, like other Art Nouveau designers, was concerned with the total environment and paid as much attention to furnishings and interior details as to the outer shell.

Below right and bottom The study and two views of the so-called 'Snail' room presented by Carlo Bugatti at the Turin International Exhibition of 1902. These rooms are the ultimate refinement of Bugatti's inventiveness as a furniture designer and in the fluidity of form and line which he has achieved reflect the influence of Art Nouveau. The natural coloured vellum was richly decorated with formalized plant or insect motifs painted in pastel colours and heightened with elaborate gilding.

Left A highly decorative cabinet designed by Carlo Bugatti, c.1900. Decorated with inlays of wood and metal, the flat surfaces of this piece are covered in vellum, a material which Bugatti was to use increasingly until 1902 when he covered the entire surface of his furniture in vellum, concealing structure and emphasizing the fluidity of his forms. Earlier pieces, this cabinet included, show strong middle-eastern influences.

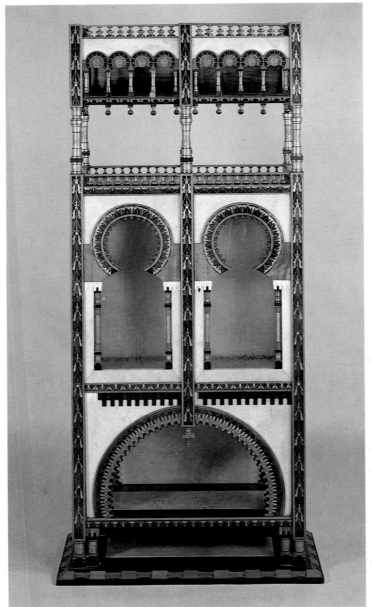

1900-1920
Arts and Crafts

The Arts and Crafts Movement had its origins in England; its influence was to extend internationally, however, and many major developments in modern furniture, above all the explosion of creativity that marked the emergence of the Modern Movement at the Bauhaus, owe a great deal to the impetus and ideologies of the British Arts and Crafts designers. Scandinavian Modernism could be regarded as the most democratically effective application of the principles of Arts and Crafts, while the current concern with hand-crafted objects might be seen as a reawakening of the ideal.

The Arts and Crafts idea started as a philosophy, but soon became a style, as designers, manufacturers and retailers capitalized on the popularity of the craft look, in many cases forgetting the teachings of John Ruskin or William Morris which were at its source. Or else the philosophy became a social stance, an attitude well expressed by Sir John Betjeman in his definition of the two poles of Edwardian architecture. 'There were,' he wrote, 'two sorts of Edwardian architect, the tweedy and the silk-hatted. The tweedy were the followers of William Morris and the Art Workers' Guild. They wore ties in a gold ring and saxe-blue shirts. They liked to live in the country and they enjoyed carpentry, joinery, blacksmith's work and doing water colours. Their Bible was *The Studio*.'

William Morris was possibly the most influential guiding spirit of Arts and Crafts and in his own work demonstrates the inherent contradictions

Embroidered crewel-work hanging, designed by William Morris in 1877 for Smeaton Manor, built by Philip Webb in 1876, and worked by Mrs Ada Phoebe Godman.

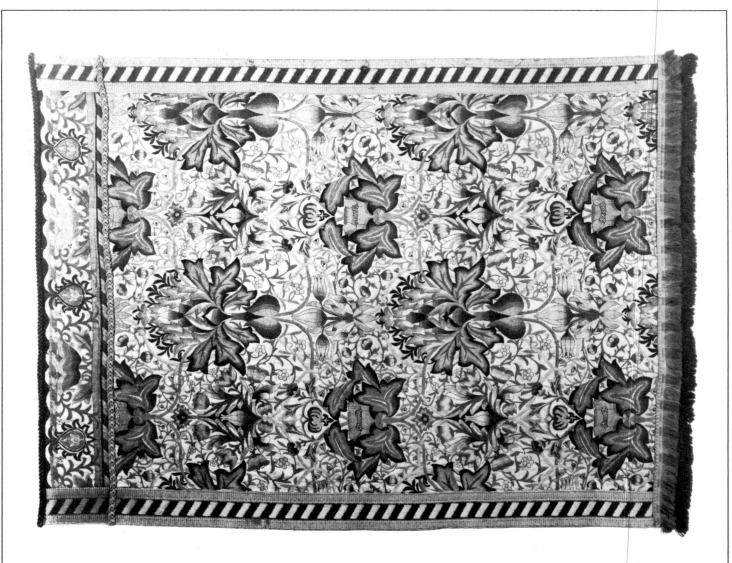

and fallacies in the philosophies which he preached and endeavoured to put into practice. Morris was a crusader who saw industrialization as the greatest potential threat to the decorative arts and who, reacting against the debilitating effect on the decorative arts of mechanized production and stylistic historicism, sought salvation in an idealistic return to the hallowed status of the crafts in the medieval age. Morris and his followers cherished the image of the medieval craft guild and several co-operatives were established in emulation of these ancient guilds, notably the Century Guild, founded in 1882 by Arthur Heygate Mackmurdo, the Art Workers' Guild, founded in 1884, and the Guild of Handicraft, founded in 1888 by Charles Robert Ashbee.

William Morris died in 1896, yet no history of twentieth-century furniture would be complete without an appreciation of his influence. Morris presented himself as a Utopian and as a socialist; he preached an ideal of '... art made by the people and for the people, a joy to the maker and the user.' Yet in his own work, through the decorating firm which he had established in 1861, he became an élitist in spite of himself, for the loving hand work which he advocated became the privilege of the wealthy minority who could afford it. Morris scorned the one solution which was possible if good design were to reach a wide public in an increasingly industrial age – the development of a harmonious relationship between artist and industry, the acceptance and exploitation of the machine.

Below Morris & Co. rush-seated 'Sussex' chair, one of various models produced by the company.

Left Decorated 'Gothic' sideboard designed by Philip Webb for Morris & Co., c.1862.

Arts and Crafts 2

Right Cabinet designed by
Ernest Gimson using
contrasting woods to create a
checker design. Gimson was
perhaps the most talented
designer of furniture among
the group that came together
as the Cotswold school.

Below The dining room of
'The Orchard', Chorley Wood,
designed in 1900 by Charles
Annesley Voysey, a leading
figure in the development of
British domestic architecture
and in the development of the
Arts and Crafts style in
furniture and interior design.

By 1900, though Morris's philosophy was still very
much alive, the Arts and Crafts style had developed
along various, not always satisfactory paths.
Several domestic architects and furniture designers aimed at and achieved a simple, honest and
sound style, using traditional, unpretentious materials in unassuming, often rustic designs. Among
them were, notably, Charles Annesley Voysey and
M.H. Baillie Scott in England and Gustav Stickley
in the United States. Others developed the notion
of creative craft work in a more complex, more
luxurious style, creating examples of fine cabinet-
making which in no way contributed to the
solution of the problems which the movement had
sought to resolve. Notable amongst this category
was the so-called Cotswold school of cabinet-
makers which included Ernest Gimson and Sidney
and Ernest Barnsley.

Finally, and regrettably, many designers and
manufacturers failed to distinguish between the
superficial, recognizable symbols of the Arts and
Crafts style and the ideals which shaped these
symbols and so the distinctive signs of hand work
were adopted as part of a fashionable visual
language.

In furniture, these often awkward surface symbols of hand work, of honest craft labour, included
elaborate wrought-iron hinges or lockplates, *repoussé* metal panels, wicker seating and uncon-
cealed joinery.

Oak armchair with leather
seat designed by Charles
Annesley Voysey, *c.*1906–10.
The simple construction and
practical materials make this a
sound and sturdy design.

United Kingdom **Voysey**

Right Oak chair designed by Charles Annesley Voysey for the Essex & Suffolk Insurance Co. premises, Chapel House, London, c.1909.

Below Sideboard designed by Charles Annesley Voysey, c.1900.

Below right Oak chair with rush seat designed by Charles Annesley Voysey, c.1904.

One of the more refreshing figures in the story of the British Arts and Crafts Movement was the domestic architect and designer Charles Annesley Voysey whose avowed intention to 'live and work in the present' distinguished him from Morris and his colleagues with their romantic yearning for the past and their archaeological eclecticism. Voysey, born in 1857, was already of a younger generation. He set up his own practice in 1882 after an apprenticeship with J.P. Seddon and built his first house in 1888. From 1882 he had been designing fabrics and wallpapers and developed a proto-Art Nouveau style, fresher, lighter, more stylized and less fussy than the complex patterns of Morris. For his furniture he favoured oak and he devised simple, sturdy forms for seat, table and cabinet designs. He made a speciality of fretted copper appliques. Voysey's furniture was just one in-gredient of his cohesive interior schemes, perhaps the most successful of which were the schemes for his own home, 'The Orchard' at Chorley Wood, Hertfordshire, built in 1900. Here can be seen the honest simplicity preached by Arts and Crafts theorists but so seldom effectively put into telling and intelligent practice.

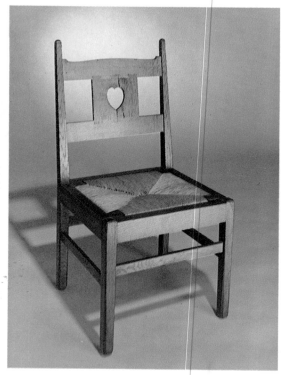

Opposite The 'Kelmscott Chaucer' cabinet, 1899, designed by Charles Annesley Voysey in oak with fretted brass decoration. A rich example of Voysey's style, the cabinet was designed to house the edition of Chaucer published by William Morris's Kelmscott Press and stands as a symbol of the Arts and Crafts Movement.

Baillie Scott

A contemporary of Voysey's and a central figure in the British Arts and Crafts Movement was architect-designer Mackay Hugh Baillie Scott. Baillie Scott was, like Voysey, primarily a domestic architect and, again like Voysey, concerned with every aspect of domestic design in pursuit of an organic sense of unity within his projects. He had a fondness for exposed beams, wood panelling and built-in seating in hearth or inglenook; he is rightly credited with having created a particular concept of the British suburban home.

His first major project was his own home, The Red House, Douglas, Isle of Man, built in 1892. Baillie Scott's most distinctive style was strongly rustic in character and oak was his favoured wood.

A typical design was his 'Manx' piano, an upright with a casing of oak, sturdily constructed and with exaggerated metalwork hinges as a modest concession to decoration. Less typical, though more distinguished, were the designs for furnishings for the palace of the Grand Duke of Hesse at Darmstadt. These more elaborately decorative designs of 1898, which included a music cabinet with stylized floral and checker motifs, were made up in the workshops of Ashbee's Guild of Handicraft. From 1898 Baillie Scott designed furniture which was manufactured by John White and sold through Liberty & Co. Both Baillie Scott and Voysey exemplified the common-sense aspects of the Arts and Crafts Movement.

Above Chair designed by M.H. Baillie Scott for the palace at Darmstadt. A stylish design though, in its emphasis on decoration, uncharacteristic of Baillie Scott's work. This chair and other furnishings created for Darmstadt by British designers reflect the strong impact made on German theorists and designers by the ideals and achievements of the British Arts and Crafts Movement. The chair was made in the workshops of the Guild of Handicraft, c.1898.

Above right Music Room project by M.H. Baillie Scott published in Germany by Alexander Koch and clearly demonstrating Baillie Scott's characteristic approach to domestic designs. He leaned heavily on rustic motifs and references but achieved harmonious results. Published 1902.

Left The 'Manx' piano designed by M.H. Baillie Scott, constructed in oak, the beloved wood of the British Arts and Crafts Movement, c.1900.

C.R. Ashbee, primarily involved in the craft of silver, also turned his attention to furniture, working in a decorative version of the Arts and Crafts style. The movement, meanwhile, had found an influential advocate in William Richard Lethaby, appointed joint principal of the newly-founded Central School in 1896 and, in 1900, appointed as the first Professor of Design at the Royal College of Art. Although the Central was founded to 'encourage the industrial application of decorative art', Lethaby's influence, however refreshing, was in the craft rather than the industrial sector and his own furniture designs bear little relevance to the true needs of the machine age, though guided by 'the seed of truth'.

Oak piano designed by Charles Robert Ashbee c.1898, incorporating chevron banding and inset plaques in translucent enamels. Ashbee's name is associated above all with the design of elegant silverware, though he proved himself capable of designing handsome furnishings.

Liberty/Heal's

Below Dressing table and wash stand manufactured for Liberty & Co. c.1900 and probably designed by Leonard Wyburd. These over-scaled designs incorporate many features from the repertoire of Arts and Crafts furniture design. Constructed in oak and of simple, sturdy design, they are decorated with stencilled canvas, pewter inlays and self-consciously rustic pegging.

Opposite above Drawing room decorated by Liberty & Co. c.1900. The firm has come to be associated most strongly with an Arts and Crafts style, but the Regent Street shop in fact provided an extensive decorating service in a variety of other styles.

Opposite below Oak chair made by William Birch, a manufacturer strongly associated with a simple, rustic Arts and Crafts style, c.1907.

Most prominent in the commercial propagation of Arts and Crafts style furniture was the Regent Street firm of Liberty & Co, founded by entrepreneur Arthur Lazenby Liberty. Liberty & Co retailed the work of independent designers, in many instances work specially commissioned for the firm, and work manufactured in Liberty's own furniture workshops. Liberty's Furniture and Decoration Studio had been established in 1883 under the direction of Leonard F. Wyburd and the firm's first cabinet workshops, started in 1887, were to remain in operation until 1940. Liberty's maintained a policy of anonymity with their designers, preferring to emphasize the image of the shop rather than the individual personality of the artist. It has been possible nonetheless, to attribute some of the most striking Liberty Arts and Crafts furniture to Leonard Wyburd. His style is wilfully rustic and he employed such decorative features as dowel handles, pewter inlays, stencilled canvas panelling and the ubiquitous rush seating.

Voysey and the Scot George Walton were among the prominent designers whose work was sold by Liberty. One of the most interesting furniture designers whose work was retailed by the Regent Street shop was E.G. Punnett, who in 1901 joined the furniture-making firm of William Birch. Punnett designed handsome furniture in walnut or the more fashionable rustic oak in a distinctive style which combined a sturdy basic construction with restrained Art Nouveau decorative inlays.

Ambrose Heal, of the London firm of Heal's, was responsible for furniture designs from the first decades of the century which demonstrated a functionalist application of the principles of the Arts and Crafts Movement. The results, while eminently practical, were depressingly spartan. Heal's had published their first catalogue of 'Plain Oak Furniture' in 1898, and their most significant contribution to the story of British furniture was in bringing straightforward, sound and functional furniture to a wide public at accessible prices. Gordon Russell was to persevere in the democratic approach pioneered by Ambrose Heal.

Liberty/Heal's

Below top Wardrobe manufactured by Liberty & Co. and designed by Leonard Wyburd, *c.*1900. Constructed in walnut with decorative inlays in other woods and metal.

Below bottom Chest of drawers manufactured by Heal's, London, early twentieth century.

Cotswold School

Below Cabinet designed by Ernest Gimson for Kenton, c.1891.

Below right top Revolving bookcase designed by Sidney Barnsley c.1913.

Below right bottom Walnut cabinet made by Peter van der Waals c.1925. Waals was a fine craftsman who made up furniture to his own designs and also made up pieces designed by Ernest Gimson, continuing to do so after that designer's death.

The craft for craft's sake aspect of the Arts and Crafts Movement found able advocates in the furniture designers and artisans of the Cotswold school. Ernest Gimson and Sidney and Ernest Barnsley had come together in the firm of Kenton & Co., set up in 1890 and which had included W.R. Lethaby as one of its founder members. Gimson and the Barnsleys moved to the Cotswolds in 1894 and from there to Daneway House, Sapperton, Gloucestershire in 1902 with Peter van der Waals, a Dutch cabinet-maker who had joined the group in 1901.

Theirs was a noble, if somewhat insular, approach to furniture design and manufacture, respectful of but never enslaved by tradition. Pevsner has described Gimson, figurehead of the group, as 'the greatest English artist-craftsman.' The description is erroneous in one respect for, despite a sympathetic appreciation of the qualities and limitations of his materials, Gimson, like Ernest Barnsley, was not a proficient craftsman,

but entrusted the implementation of his ideas to skilled artisans, including Waals, who continued to make up his designs after his death in 1919.

The group's ambition, as expressed by Gimson, was to produce furniture that was 'useful and right, pleasantly shaped and finished, good enough, but not too good for ordinary use.' They favoured native woods, walnut in particular and the almost inevitable oak. Champfered edges were a hallmark of their style and elegantly softened the lines of their furniture.

Gimson was responsible also for a number of prestige pieces, usually cabinets on open bases, which must rank as perhaps the most beautiful examples of British cabinet-making of the early part of the twentieth century. For these he used more exotic materials, rich woods including ebony with fruitwood marquetry and inlays of mother-of-pearl and ivory. The decorative motifs were either abstract patterns or stylized plant forms.

The British Arts and Crafts Movement found adherents also in Glasgow, where Mackintosh's earlier, more traditional style proved influential through the late nineties and the early years of the twentieth century. As he developed his individualistic style, however, Mackintosh left his more conservative contemporaries behind. The Glasgow school included George Walton, who had collaborated with Mackintosh in the furnishing and decoration of Miss Cranston's Buchanan Street Tearoom in 1897-8, George Logan and E.A. Taylor, both of whom designed for the decorating firm of Wylie and Lockhead. Glasgow furniture had its distinctive features, more in the decorative details, however, such as the formalized roses so strongly associated with the school, than in any novel ideas in construction. The group did, however, strongly influence some pioneers of modern design in Germany and Austria and can thus claim a permanent position in international design.

Above Bookcase designed by George Logan and manufactured by Wylie & Lockhead, c.1900. Mahogany with carved and inlaid decoration incorporating mother-of-pearl, white metal mounts, leather inserts and leaded glass doors.

Above left Armchair designed by George Walton c.1900 and made in oak with rush seating.

Left Interior designed by George Walton for the new Brompton Road showrooms of Kodak, c.1905.

United States

In the United States the Arts and Crafts Movement flourished from the early nineties until about 1915. In his catalogue of the travelling exhibition, 'The Arts and Crafts Movement in America 1876–1916', editor Robert Judson Clark takes 1893 as a turning point, the year in which Greene and Greene arrived in Pasadena, in which Frank Lloyd Wright set up his own practice and the year of the World's Columbian Exposition in Chicago. With the bankrupcy declaration in 1915 of Gustav Stickley's enterprises and the closure, after its December 1916 issue, of the *Craftsman* magazine, the American movement died a natural death.

The American Arts and Crafts Movement drew on the ideology of British designers, several of whom, including Walter Crane and C.R. Ashbee had travelled in the United States and given first-hand inspiration to local craftsmen. The nineties

saw the establishment of societies along the lines of British precursors. The Minneapolis Chalk and Chisel Club founded in 1895 became the Arts and Crafts Society in 1899.

In 1897 the Boston Society of Arts and Crafts and the Chicago Arts and Crafts Society were set up, while in the same year the first major American Arts and Crafts Exhibition was staged at Copley Hall in Boston. In 1900 the Guild of Arts and Crafts was organized in New York. Other societies followed, including a William Morris Society, founded in 1903 in Chicago to commemorate the father of the Movement.

The central figure in the story of American Arts and Crafts furniture was Gustav Stickley. In 1898 he set up his Gustav Stickley Company, travelled extensively in Europe, meeting leading figures in progressive furniture design and returned to start work in the severe style which he was to popularize under the trademark of 'Craftsman' furniture. Stickley used straight planks in designs of a remarkable sobriety. He explained, 'When I first began to use the severely plain, structural forms, I chose oak as the wood that, above all others, was adapted to massive simplicity of construction . . . (to the) strong straight lines and plain surfaces of the furniture.'

Stickley extended his activities to publishing with the appearance in October 1901 of the first issue of the *Craftsman*, a monthly magazine which, in turn, helped spread the taste for his style of furniture and emphasized the trade name, a valuable contribution in the face of competition from various manufacturers, including his own brothers who were, of course, able to capitalize on the family name.

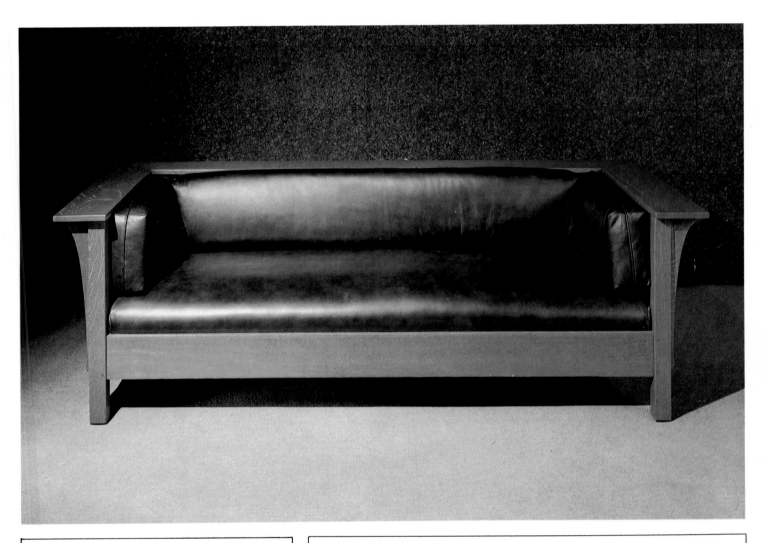

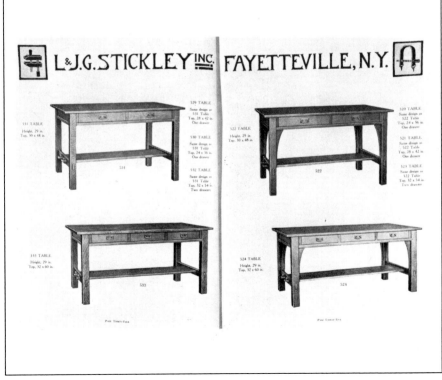

Rohlfs/Ellis

In his small Buffalo workshops, from about 1890, Charles Rohlfs created simple oak furniture with such distinctive and self-conscious Arts and Crafts features as pegged joints. Harvey Ellis designed a range of oak furniture with restrained floral inlays in the Scottish style, first advertised in the July 1903 issue of *Craftsman*. In the early years of the century the Roycroft workshops at East Aurora, N.Y. produced a range of oak furniture in what has been described as a '... sincere, if sometimes plebeian, version of the ideals of William Morris.' The Roycroft artistic community was led by Elbert Hubbard, an enthusiastic disciple of Morris.

In the mid-west the most influential figure, an architect of exceptional vision and humanity, was Frank Lloyd Wright. His furniture designs were related to specific architectural contexts and played well-defined rhythmic roles within the totality of his interior schemes. In his pursuit of simplicity and his early preference for oak Wright followed a similar path to other contemporaries but his independence of spirit places him in a category apart from the fashionable Arts and Crafts style of Stickley and the like.

Right Carved oak chair designed by Charles Rohlfs, *c*.1898. This chair, created by Rohlfs for his own living room, is a remarkable example of Art Nouveau in the flowing lines of the tall back, carved by George Thiele.

Below Magazine rack designed and manufactured in the workshops of the Roycroft community, *c.*1908–12.

Below Chair in oak with leather seating and brass studs, designed and manufactured in the workshops of the Roycroft community, *c.*1908–12.

Greene & Greene

The Arts and Crafts Movement in furniture design found two sophisticated exponents on the West Coast in the architects, brothers Charles and Henry Greene. Their reputation rests on the creation of four remarkable private houses in the period 1907-9. The furniture which they designed to complete the interiors was meticulously executed by cabinet-maker Peter Hall and was characterized by the use of richly polished hardwoods, especially walnut or mahogany, by softened edges and discreet stepped motifs which gave a slightly Chinese character, and by the focus of attention on raised pegheads.

Above and right Details of furniture and panelling in the Gamble House at Pasadena, designed and decorated in 1908 by the Greene brothers. The hallmarks of their distinctive style included the softened edges to the richly polished walnut visible in these views, raised peg heads and stepped details in Chinese taste.

In the Scandinavian countries the Arts and Crafts idea was applied to furniture as to other aspects of design without fuss and without stylistic pretention, not as a passing fashion but as part of a sincere, and effectual, attempt to democratize decent design. The Scandinavians have traditionally respected the craft of wood rather as a pleasing natural furnishing material than as an excuse for the display of virtuosity. The human scale was never forgotten nor was the liberal socialist ideal of good design for all. Danish designer Kay Bojesen stated that 'The things we make should have life and heart in them . . . they must be human, vital and warm.' In 1917 the Svenska Slöjdsföreningen organized a competition for the design of low-cost furnishings, anticipating by three decades the Museum of Modern Art's 'Low Cost Furniture' competition.

The aim, democratic and idealistic, was 'to stimulate the production of types and models suited to mass-production and therefore inexpensive, yet in good taste.' The Scandinavian furniture industry established its guilds, supervising bodies and societies along the lines of British Arts and Crafts Guilds; but whereas the British guilds had, for the most part, in the words of one critic ' . . . spawned a progeny of cranks and eccentrics, the "arty-crafty" with their aura of the homespun . . .', the Scandinavian bodies established the firm basis of logic and humanism which was to make the Scandinavian image so internationally influential after the Second World War.

In Denmark, the most influential figure was designer and teacher Kaare Klint who in 1934 was appointed lecturer in the newly formed department of furniture within the Copenhagen Academy of Art. Even before this date, however, Klint had started his anthropomorphic research into the most practical and natural forms and proportions for furniture.

The Svenska Slöjdsföreningen has a long his-tory, dating back to the mid nineteenth century. Its influence was to become discernible by the turn of the century, promoting a dictum of sound design which today seems self evident but which eighty years ago was a noble ambition, the ambition that '. . . everything should answer the purpose it was intended for. A chair should be comfortable to sit on, a table comfortable to work, or eat at, a bed good to sleep in.' In Norway, the Brukskunst, Applied Art Association, was founded along similar lines in 1918, while Finnish furniture design benefited from a craft revival dating back to the seventies, the Central School of Arts and Crafts being founded in Helsinki in 1871, bringing into being a first generation of designers who were to create the climate of concern both for craft and aesthetics and for human values which was to encourage the work of Alvar Aalto and the significant contemporary renaissance of Finnish craft.

The Arts and Crafts Movement was a socio-cultural phenomenon beset with unresolved contradictions, but nonetheless a collective ideo-logical manifestation which, interpreted by such perceptive designers or critics as Henry Van de Velde or Herman Muthesius was to prove of considerable relevance in the formulation of a modern school of furniture design.

Below top Folding stool designed by Kaare Klint in the thirties in ash with sailcloth seat. The Arts and Crafts ideals were implemented in Scandinavia in an unassuming but effective way. Kaare Klint was a prominent figure in preparing the way for the international supremacy of the Scandinavian image after the Second World War.

Left Desk in Cuban mahogany designed by Kaare Klint in 1933.

1900-1920
Modernism: Beginnings

Modernism, an attitude to design which had already established a pre-history of ideologies through the second half of the nineteenth century, took root around 1900 as a progressive alternative both to the escapism of the Arts and Crafts style in its more cosy, pseudo-rustic manifestations and to the luxurious, élitist extremes of the high Art Nouveau style. In the words of Nikolaus Pevsner, historian of the evolution of modern design, 'Honesty and saneness became the ideals that replaced the sultry dreams of Art Nouveau aesthetics.' Modernism was to become the aesthetic of the machine age, with functionalism and design rationalism as prominent ideals. Much of the theory of Modernism was closely related to rationales of the emergent concept of industrial design, today a well-established area of design aesthetics, but at the turn of the century still an area of often uneasy compromises.

Despite its overt basis of functionalism and truth to materials and its ideal of industrialized series production for the dissemination of intelligent design along liberal-socialist lines, Modernism became just as much a pursuit of style as a pursuit of logic. The major exponents of the style as it evolved between the wars and its most prominent precursors were evidently concerned to express their ideals through a series of design features, the value of which was symbolic rather than functional.

A clear example of this pattern of thought can be seen in the deliberate cult around 1900 of the rectilinear as expressing a greater structural logic, and also as a defiant contrast to the emphatically curvilinear Art Nouveau style. In the hands of designers internationally, however, from Frank Lloyd Wright to Charles Rennie Mackintosh, the straight line became exaggerated as a design feature.

Modernism in furniture design was, for the most part, the by-product of the emergence of the Modern Movement in architecture and the most exciting precursors of Modernist furniture design were architects anxious to apply their principles at every level from the structural, architectural shell to each detail of interior furnishings and fittings; to quote Pevsner again, 'The Modern Movement in architecture, in order to be fully expressive of the twentieth century had to possess both qualities – the faith in science and technology, in social science and rational planning, and the romantic faith in speed and the roar of machines.' The same words might well be used to express the Modernist ideal in furniture design, an ideal which has been

pursued in every way, even to the extreme of the 'streamlined' furniture created in the thirties, giving absurdly to static objects forms expressive of this 'romantic faith in speed.'

A key figure in the formulation of the Modernist aesthetic was Hermann Muthesius, the German architect and civil servant who spent several years from 1896 in England and returned to Germany to publish an extensive survey of the British Arts and Crafts Movement and of progressive British domestic design. Muthesius perceived the essentially conservative character of the Arts and Crafts Movement, saw its emphasis on craft tradition as being just as unconstructive as the stylistic eclecticism and historicism of German manufacturers. Muthesius demanded 'perfect and pure utility', attracted kindred spirits and was instrumental in the establishment in 1907 of the Deutscher Werkbund.

Germany became the true fatherland of Modernism, for it was in Germany that architects and designers most consistently eschewed the temptations of decoration in pursuit of pure design, grouping themselves in schools and co-operative groups which included notably the Vereinigte Deutsche Werkstätten in Munich, the Deutscher Werkbund in Dresden, and the Kunstgewerbes-chule at Weimar which was to become the Bauhaus in 1919 and from which was to emerge the most clearly distilled version of Modernism as the fruit of the collective efforts of forward-looking minds.

Germany's pioneers of Modernism acknowledged their debt to British theorists and designers, respecting above all the restraint and simplicity of the best of British Arts and Crafts. With one brilliant exception, however, British designers failed for the most part to escape the retrospective aspects of the Arts and Crafts Movement. The exception was the Glasgow architect-designer Charles Rennie Mackintosh who created a sophisticated, highly individual style of furniture and in turn strongly influenced the development of a rectilinear aesthetic in Vienna. Vienna was another key centre for the exploration of a nascent Modernism, though the artists of the Vienna school, grouped first as the Wiener Secession and subsequently as the Wiener Werkstätte, were rarely to abandon their interest in the decorative aspects of design and, indeed, after an initial flurry of rectilinear purity in the early years of the century which seemed to mark the Viennese, led notably by Josef Hoffman and Koloman Moser, as true precursors of Modernism, the Werkstätte lapsed into a primarily decorative aesthetic.

Below An executive office within the Larkin Administration Building designed by Frank Lloyd Wright in 1904 and claimed to be the first office designed with purpose-made metal furniture

United Kingdom **Mackintosh 1**

An exploratory Modernism provided a stepping stone into the twentieth century at a time when the decorative excesses of curvilinear Art Nouveau were the height of fashion but destined equally soon to become outmoded. Forward-looking designers internationally sought a new style and there emerged several distinct styles as precursors of Modernism, each with its national and personal characteristics.

Few figures of this period had the rare combination of humanism, spatial sense and sophistication that made of Charles Rennie Mackintosh one of the most fascinating designers of his era.

It remains, however, very difficult to convey in words the true spirit of Mackintosh's furniture designs and of the interiors for which the furniture was created. It is easy to list his achievements, less easy to express fully their character, since he was master of the abstract as well as the tangible materials of furniture design. Mackintosh used the space around and within his structures and the light that fell on and passed through them as compositional elements just as important as wood or fabric.

In fact, though his contribution to the history of design was considerable, the lack of understanding shown towards Mackintosh's work, narrowing the field of sympathetic patrons, considerably limited his output. Foremost among his patrons was Miss Cranston, for whom he decorated a series of Glasgow tearooms and whose home, Hous'hill, he refurbished from 1904. Other important patrons were William Davidson, for whom he designed and decorated Windyhill around 1900, and Walter Blackie, for whom Mackintosh created his most ambitious and most expressive private house, Hill House, of 1903–4, with its celebrated white bedroom as a remarkable and highly refined celebration of Mackintosh's most sophisticated style. Much of Mackintosh's earlier furniture has a sturdy character very much in keeping with Scottish tradition and stained oak was the favoured wood. His lofty high-back chair of 1897 for Miss Cranston's Argyl Street Tearoom was a landmark in his development of the refinement which found its apogee in such schemes as the Hill House white bedroom, the Room de Luxe of the Willow Tearooms and his projects of 1901 for the *Haus Eines Kunstfreundes* competition sponsored by Alexander Koch in Darmstadt.

Below The Music Room at Hous'hill. This interior by Charles Rennie Mackintosh was part of an extensive project to refurbish the interior of the home of one of his most important patrons, Miss Cranston, 1904.

Right A ladderback chair in ebonized wood. One of a pair designed by Charles Rennie Mackintosh to be set in the White Bedroom of his most ambitious and most distinguished private house project, Hill House, of 1903–4.

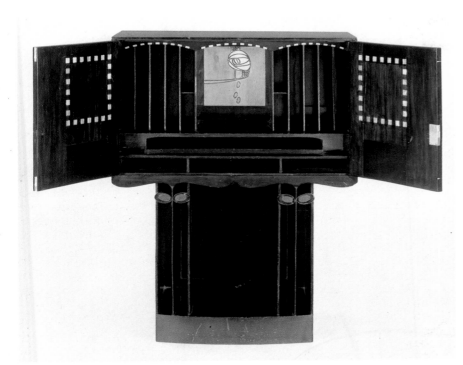

Left Writing desk designed by Charles Rennie Mackintosh and made for his personal use. The design was conceived in 1904 as part of the furnishings for Hill House. The desk was executed in an uncharacteristic dark stained wood with decorative inlays of mother-of-pearl and ivory and with a decorative back panel of leaded glass set in a sheet of metal. For many years, after its purchase from the Mackintosh Memorial Exhibition in 1933, the desk was in the possession of Allan Ure, until its sale at Sotheby's in 1979 for a record price for any item of twentieth-century furniture of £80,000. (See also frontispiece).

Below The White Bedroom at Hill House, designed by Charles Rennie Mackintosh, 1903–4 and undoubtedly one of his most refined and successful interior schemes.

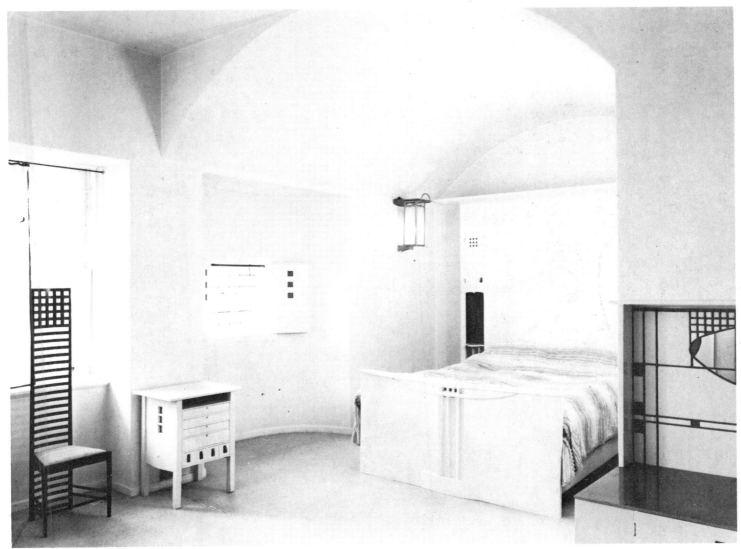

Mackintosh 2

Below left Armchair designed by Charles Rennie Mackintosh for the Music Room of Miss Cranston's home, Hous'hill, 1904. The oval motifs between the upright splats are of lilac glass, a typical detail.

Below right Upright cabinet designed by Charles Rennie Mackintosh for the Blue Bedroom, Hous'hill, 1904. Oak with leaded glass recess and inlay of mother-of-pearl.

Mackintosh was the guiding spirit of a small group of designers who had met as students at the Glasgow School of Art and who became known as the 'Glasgow Four'. The other three were Herbert McNair and the sisters Margaret and Frances MacDonald who married Mackintosh and McNair respectively. McNair designed furniture and interior schemes in a personal version of the Glasgow style, but still strongly reflecting the influence of his more gifted colleague.

Few other British designers around the turn of the century escaped either the rustic character of the Arts and Crafts style, the historicism of traditional Edwardian styles or the superficial decorative features of Art Nouveau to achieve the elegant functional discipline and restraint of a more truly modern style. In a survey, 'Modern British Domestic Architecture and Decoration', published by *The Studio* in 1901, were one or two schemes, however, shown side by side with the more usual sturdy oak, which suggest that Mackintosh was not entirely alone as a British precursor of Modernism. Most interesting were the designs by architect Charles Annesley Voysey for the furnishings of 'The Orchard', Chorley Wood. Voysey's elegant austerity in such details as the screens and stair rails of plain vertical slats and the attenuated lines of high-back chairs or bed posts distinguishes this work from his more usual Arts and Crafts style.

Slender verticals and plain white panelling were used to great effect by designer G.M. Ellwood in a drawing-room, published in this same survey, with thin-limbed mahogany furniture upholstered in mauve and grey silk or velvet. Ellwood's schemes, however, and, despite his undoubted importance as a domestic architect, even Voysey's projects, lack the single-minded, visionary character of Mackintosh's work.

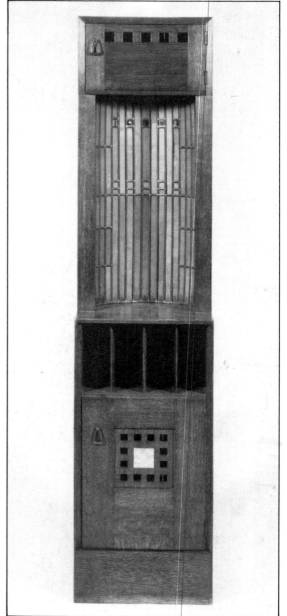

Left Drawing room designed by G.M. Ellwood for J.S. Henry Esq. and illustrated in the 1901 *Studio* publication, 'Modern British Domestic Architecture and Decoration'. The designer has achieved a harmonious blend of clean lines and a sense of lightness with a certain indulgence in aestheticism in the decorative details, colours and fabrics.

Below The hall of 'The Orchard', Chorley Wood, designed by Charles Annesley Voysey and perhaps this designer's most succesful attempt at a style which escapes the cloying rusticity of so much of Arts and Crafts and moves towards a more modern style in which light and space are ingredients. 1900.

United States **Wright**

Below right Frank Lloyd Wright's 'Cube' chair of *c*.1895 and described by the designer's son, John, as the first piece of modern furniture designed in the United States. For its date, it is certainly a quite remarkable exercise in uncompromising and undecorated angularity.

Bottom Oak print table designed by Frank Lloyd Wright for the Francis W. Little house, Peoria, Illinois, 1903.

A major figure in the evolution of Modernism was American architect/designer Frank Lloyd Wright. Wright also was a visionary and an individualist who evolved a distinctive style in the 1890s. This was a mellow, humanistic Modernism which he was to develop and refine, with little regard for passing fads or fashions, through more than half a century until his death in 1959. Wright's rooms are

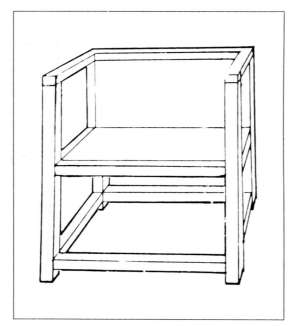

always immensely inviting and he never abandoned his respect for natural colours and materials, especially wood and stone in his domestic schemes, even around 1930 when the new language of International Modernism called for cold metal and glass. An early landmark in Wright's career and in the story of modern furniture was his cube chair of *c*.1895, a remarkable design for its date which has been described by his son, John, as 'The first piece of modern furniture made in this country.'

Wright appreciated the potential of using his furniture to express function and define space. This can be seen in his use of the high backs of dining chairs to serve almost as screens, delineating one space, the eating area, within the larger space of a room. In 1895 for the Oak Park House, Illinois, he designed tall chair backs of upright slats and in 1908 took the idea a stage further in the dining chairs for the Frederick C. Robie house, Chicago, in which the back splats were extended down to the ground, emphasizing their symbolic value in the definition of space.

The versatile Wright was just as much a pioneer in the design of furniture for the work as for the domestic context. He broke new ground in the furnishings of his Larkin Administration Building of 1904, a project which has been described as 'an industrial cathedral that should have delighted Viollet Le Duc' and for which he designed what he claimed to be the first metal office furniture.

Above left Child's chair designed by Frank Lloyd Wright for the Avery Coonley Playhouse, Riverside, Illinois, in 1912. The emphatic angularity of this design bears little relation to functional concerns, other than simplicity of manufacture, and shows, as with so many proto-Modernist designs, a concern above all with expressive style.

Above Table designed in 1904 by Frank Lloyd Wright and again demonstrating the purely stylistic obsession with attenuated verticals, the function of which is symbolic.

Left Office desk with swivel seat designed in 1904 by Frank Lloyd Wright for the Larkin Administration offices and thought to be the first all-metal design for office furniture. This functionalist design, clumsy perhaps to today's sophisticated eye, is nonetheless a design landmark of considerable importance.

Germany **Darmstadt**

In Germany and Austria the development of Modernism depended on group rather than isolated individual contributions, though inevitably the most eloquent spokesmen and most gifted designers distinguished themselves within the various groups. The group approach was particularly strong in Germany, attracting the most progressive and persuasive theorists who, in the rapid industrial expansion of the years before the First World War, saw the need for the development of a new aesthetic for industrial production. German designers toyed briefly with curvilinear Art Nouveau, the motifs of which were propagated in the late nineties by such new art journals as *Pan*, *Jugend*, from which German Art Nouveau or Jugendstil took its name, *Deutsche Kunst und Dekoration*, and *Dekorative Kunst*.

The fashion was short-lived in progressive circles, however, and even designers more concerned with domestic decoration than with industrial design evolved a rectilinear aesthetic. An important creative centre was the artists colony founded at Darmstadt by the Duke of Hesse and which attracted among others the talents of Peter Behrens and the Austrian Joseph Olbrich. After an initial indulgence in the curvilinear, Darmstadt furniture became characterized by rectilinear construction, though distinguished by concern for craft which linked it perhaps more to the British Arts and Crafts Movement than to the emergent industrial aesthetic.

The links with British Arts and Crafts were emphasized by the invitation extended to Baillie Scott to design furniture for the palace at Darmstadt. The results were amongst his most sophisticated designs. In 1901 Behrens designed and furnished his own home at Darmstadt in a style which reflected the influence of Baillie Scott, while in 1902-3 Olbrich emphasized the Austrian influence in a richly inlaid angular suite of furniture for the music room of the new palace. The stylish furniture of designer Hans Christiansen reflects this same angular but essentially decorative Vienna influence.

Decorative cabinet designed by Baillie Scott in 1898 as part of the furnishings of the palace at Darmstadt. The cabinet was manufactured in the workshops of Charles Robert Ashbee's Guild of Handicraft.

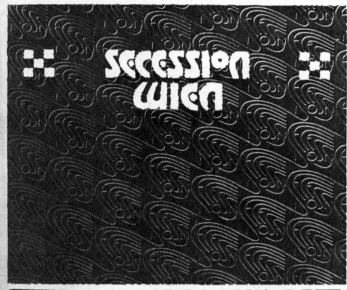

Above left Poster for the fourteenth Secessionist exhibition.

Above Cover for the May 1902 issue of *Deutsche Kunst und Dekoration* designed by Margaret Macdonald Mackintosh.

Left Suite of furniture designed by Joseph Olbrich for Darmstadt in an austere proto-Modernist style.

Deutsche Werkstätten and Deutscher Werkbund 1

More central to the evolution of a Modernist aesthetic in Germany were the activities of designers in Dresden and Weimar. Dresden had seen the foundation of a Werkstätte in 1898 by Karl Schmidt, a cabinet-maker who, in 1905, asked his brother-in-law Richard Riemerschmid to design a chair '. . . developing the style from the spirit of the machine.' It was in Dresden that the teachings of Muthesius came home to roost and Muthesius was instrumental in the foundation of the Deutscher Werkbund at Dresden in 1907.

The year 1907 has been described as 'one of the most significant in the history of industrial design,' and, indeed, in furniture design as in other areas of design, the creation of the Werkbund, an association of designers and manufacturers, the first major attempt to reconcile good design to series production, art to industry, marks an important turning point, creating the profession of the industrial designer and putting paid to the notion that good furniture design and craft execution were somehow irrevocably linked.

The membership of the Werkbund, which was by invitation, included Behrens, who in 1907 took on the role of design co-ordinator to A.E.G. and became effectively the first industrial designer in the modern sense, Richard Riemerschmid, Bruno Paul, Bernhard Pankok, Walter Gropius, Belgian architect/designer Henry Van de Velde and Austrians Josef Hoffmann and Otto Wagner. The achievements of the Werkbund were published in a

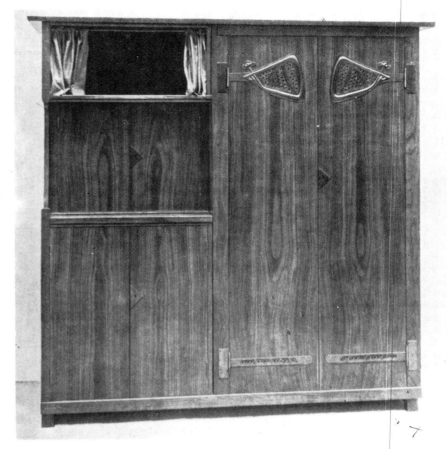

Deutsche Werkstätten and Deutscher Werkbund 1

Opposite above Cabinet designed in 1903 by W. Von Beckerath of Munich and demonstrating the increasing involvement after a brief fashion for Art Nouveau in Germany with a new rectilinear style which was to mark the transition into Modernism proper.

Opposite below The cabinet-making workshops at Hellerau of Deutscher Werkbund designer Richard Riemerschmid.

Left Upright cabinet designed by Bernhard Pankok and illustrated in the 1915 yearbook of the Deutscher Werkbund.

Deutsche Werkstätten and Deutscher Werkbund 2

series of annuals, the first of which appeared in 1912, illustrating and discussing design at every level from furniture to factory, while in 1914 the Werkbund's achievements were the subject of a major exhibition in Cologne, an event regrettably overshadowed by the outbreak of war. In retrospect, despite the persuasiveness of Werkbund theory, the group's contribution to furniture design was more in the creation of a climate between artist and manufacturer conducive to the future series production of modern designs, than in the creation of specifically significant furniture and other types of object.

At Weimar, meanwhile, Henry Van de Velde was involved in the establishment of a private craft school which in 1908 was taken over by the state as the Grossherzogliche Kunstgewerbeschule. Van de Velde stepped down as principal and recommended Walter Gropius as his successor, a fortuitous suggestion which was not in fact taken up until after the war when, in 1919, Gropius was appointed director of the school now restyled as the Staatliche Bauhaus. Here, in the Werkbund and the Weimar school, was established the ideological background which was to give Germany a dramatic lead in progressive furniture design.

Cabin Furnishings designed by Richard Riemerschmid for the *Kronprinzessin Cecilie* and illustrated in the 1914 year book of the Deutscher Werkbund.

Above Furnishings designed by Henry Van de Velde at Weimar and illustrated in the 1915 yearbook of the Deutscher Werkbund.

Left Folio cabinet designed in 1899 by Henry Van de Velde. Despite an early indulgence in curvilinear, decorative Art Nouveau, Van de Velde emerged as a key figure in the development of the Modernist aesthetic in Germany.

Austria **Wiener Werkstätte 1**

The forward-looking artists of Vienna, led by Josef Hoffmann, Koloman Moser and Joseph Olbrich had rallied together in 1897 in the foundation of the Wiener Secession. Their leaning towards a rectilinear style was consolidated in 1900 after the enthusiastic reception extended to an invitation exhibit submitted to their eighth exhibition, in the autumn of 1900, by the Glasgow Four, led by Mackintosh. The Austrians were profoundly impressed by Mackintosh's work and for a period of years adopted various features of his style, notably the rectilinear construction and his fondness for the checker pattern as a decorative motif.

In 1902 Mackintosh was invited by the wealthy Viennese businessman Fritz Warndorfer, a great patron of the Secessionists, to decorate and furnish a music room. The result was a masterful exercise in Mackintosh's precious, white mode. For the same house, Hoffmann designed a dining room. In 1903 Hoffmann and Moser, with the backing of Warndorfer, set up a craft studio, the Wiener Werkstätte, inspired by the Guild of Handicraft Ltd and with the advice and encouragement of Mackintosh.

In the years up to the first World War the Werkstätte was a fertile source of innovation in furniture design, combining rich materials and a concern for finish in severe, geometric silhouettes of an aesthetic that was dramatically rather than rationally modern. Rich veneers and inlays of mother-of-pearl characterize the work of Hoffmann and Moser in this period. Moser created the familiar chequer patterns in contrasting veneers of pale and dark woods; Hoffmann achieved a spectacular *tour-de-force* in the cigar-cabinet of 1910-14

now in the Osterreichisches Museum für Angewandte Kunst, Vienna, a striking ziggurat veneered in ebony and mother-of-pearl. The most ambitious decorative scheme undertaken by the group was the Palais Stoclet in Brussels, a sumptuous private house started in 1905, designed by Hoffmann and furnished by various members of the Werkstätte working in close collaboration under him.

Above right Smoker's cabinet faced in mother-of-pearl and ebony designed by Josef Hoffmann c.1910–14. The combination of stylish angular forms and rich materials is typical of the best products of the Wiener Werkstätte just before the First World War.

Right Charles Rennie Mackintosh's design for the Drawing/Music Room for the Haus Eines Kunstfreundes project of 1901. Plate VII from the Folio published by Alexander Koch in 1902.

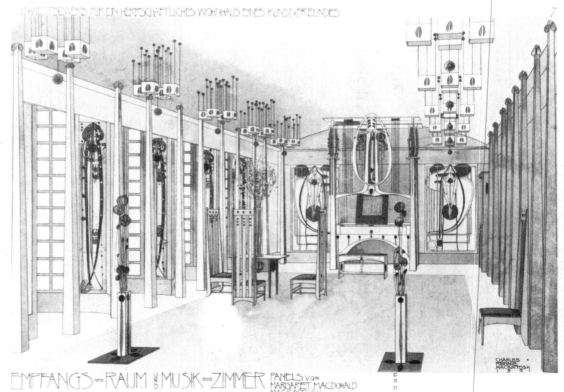

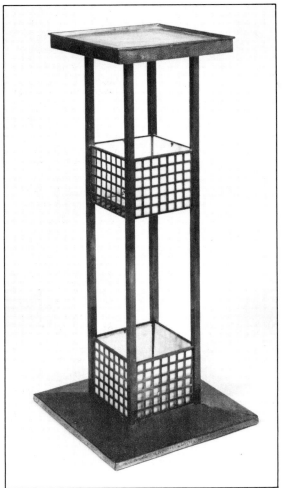

Left Table designed in 1904 by Josef Hoffmann. The elimination of decoration and the angularity of construction mark this design as a precursor of Modernism.

Above Table in perforated and beaten metal and white glass designed *c.*1905 by Josef Hoffmann. The checker pattern which is incorporated as a decorative feature of this design was one of the most obvious borrowings from Charles Rennie Mackintosh's repertoire of decorative motifs.

Above left Tub chair designed by Josef Hoffmann *c.*1901 in beech, mahogany and aluminium.

Wiener Werkstätte 2

Hoffmann and other members of the Werkstätte, as well as working on such commissions for high luxury furnishings, created new designs for series production by major industrialized furniture makers, notably for the old-established firm of Thonet and for Kohn. Two leading figures in the evolution of a self-consciously functional, less decorative version of the Vienna style were architects Otto Wagner and Adolf Loos. Wagner, born in 1841, was the elder statesman of Austrian Modernism who developed a staunch functionalism in the enlightened atmosphere of turn-of-the-century Vienna. His well-considered furniture designs for his masterly Post Office Savings Bank of 1904-6 perfectly express his rational, practical approach. Loos asserted himself as a fervent critic of ornament for its own sake and, for the most part, practised the austere functionalism and decorative restraint which he preached.

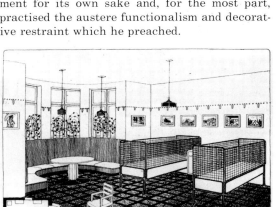

Opposite above Design for the Cabaret Fledermaus, Vienna. A typical interior scheme of the proto-Modernist Vienna school.

Opposite above left Another typical proto-Modernist project was this design by Richard Muller for a children's bedroom.

Opposite below left Buffet designed in 1901 by Koloman Moser.

Opposite below right Armchair designed by Koloman Moser in 1904. A strictly angular construction is here combined with an opulent use of materials, including rich figured wood veneer and mother-of-pearl.

Above Table and chair designed in 1902 by Adolf Loos, a designer who followed a more rigid concept of functionalism than the more decoratively-inclined Hoffmann or Moser.

Below Chair designed in 1904 by Otto Wagner for the interior of the Postal Savings Bank. Wagner, the father figure of the Vienna school, has been described as 'the missionary of the absolute primacy of structure over decoration'.

The Twenties
Art Deco

Art Deco, the style in which French *ébénisterie* asserted its international supremacy at the Paris Exposition Internationale des Arts Décoratifs et Industriels Modernes of 1925 had evolved its characteristics in the years before the hiatus of the First World War. Indeed, despite the considerable *succès de scandale* of the fanciful extremes of high Art Nouveau as exhibited in 1900, the public very soon tired of the decorative excesses of this style and even by 1905 the exuberant curves of Art Nouveau were being replaced by more restrained, more disciplined, classical lines in furniture design. Pierre Olmer in his seminal 1927 study *La Renaissance du Mobilier Français 1890–1910* illustrated a stark, completely rectilinear table of 1908 by Paul Follot, a designer who had happily indulged in the commercially successful Art Nouveau style but who, sensing the shift in the public's taste, had just as easily modified his own stylistic stance. Maurice Dufrêne, who like Follot had toyed successfully with Art Nouveau, similarly moved towards a more restrained style in the very early years of the century. Olmer illustrated, notably, a gracious and feminine bedroom by Dufrêne of 1906, marking clearly the new direction with neo-classical straight fluted legs, disciplined swags and floral details, but with just the occasional sweeping line as a lingering farewell to Art Nouveau.

Art Nouveau survived for a few years, the idiom still being present in the work of such designers as Guimard or the Nancy group, for whom the organic form was a statement of faith. But the exhibits at the annual Salon des Artistes-Décorateurs and the Salon d'Automne showed clearly that a new direction was needed.

During these transitional years, there was considerable concern among the creative French furniture designers at the increasing influx of foreign manufactured goods, a concern which was made more acute by the impressive cohesion of the Munich Werkbund's invitation exhibit at the Salon d'Automne of 1910. The unity and forward-looking attitude of the Werkbund group contrasted with the disorganized situation of the French furniture and craft industries and inspired the combined forces of the Société d'Encouragement, the Société des Artistes-Décorateurs and the Union Centrale to make an application to the French government for the organization in 1914 or 1915 of a major international exhibition which would give French designers and manufacturers an inspiring challenge to evolve a new phase in their creativity.

The exhibition, discussed as early as 1907, was to be the inspiration for a renaissance in French furniture and decorative design. Delayed by the First World War, the project which materialized finally as the 1925 Exposition Internationale des Arts Décoratifs et Industriels proved to be more a swan song than the inspirational beginnings of the renaissance that was Art Deco. By 1925 new Modernist influences were emerging in Germany, in the Netherlands and even amongst a group of French designers and architects, which emphasized the essentially traditional nature of Art Deco. Even within the luxury world of Art Deco furniture craftsmanship the influences of avant-garde art and the fascination with primitive African art were shaping a style quite different in feeling from the reassuring, essentially bourgeois style of the grand *ébénistes* of the 1925 style, Emile-Jacques Ruhlmann and Süe et Mare.

Above Marquetry panel in pure Art Deco style designed for the luxury cars of the Compagnie Internationale des Wagons-Lits in the twenties. Art Deco was a style used to luxurious effect in the decoration of these rail cars but to even greater effect in the decoration of prestige liners.

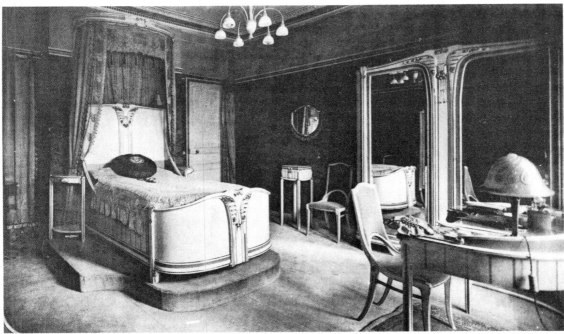

Above Carpet designed by the painter Marie Laurencin in the twenties, Laurencin collaborated on decorative schemes with the designer André Groult and her feminine, pastel patterns and motifs complemented his furniture, creating charming settings in the Art Deco style.

Above left The Grand Salon in the Pavillon d'un Collectionneur designed by Emile-Jacques Ruhlmann for the Paris International Exhibition of 1925, perhaps the most important Art Deco room featured in the exhibition.

Left Bedroom designed by Maurice Dufrêne in 1906 in a transitional style between Art Nouveau and Art Deco. There is no hint at all here of the development of Modernism.

Art Deco 2

During the twenties, countless folios and books on the contemporary decorative arts were published in France, providing an invaluable and comprehensive survey of Art Deco and the stylish Modernism which superseded it. Gaston Quenioux, Emile-Bayard, Henri Verne and René Chavance compiled particularly interesting anthologies in which the dominant features of Art Deco can be clearly recognized. Although the personalities of the foremost *ébénistes* of the period brought about recognizable individual styles, there is an overall neo-classicism in Art Deco. This classicism, the reaction to the neo-rococo curves of Art Nouveau, was to be seen in the popularity of straight, tapering and often fluted legs, and in the restrained decorative motifs. Where Art Nouveau had allowed decoration to become form, Art Deco disciplined decoration within the simple silhouette of a piece of furniture, and particularly popular were motifs from the traditional neo-classical repertoire: garlands, swags and bouquets, carved in low relief or inlaid.

Not all designers found the transition from Art Nouveau to Art Deco an easy one. The Nancy cabinet-makers, for example, who had created such a strong and satisfying version of Art Nouveau, were ill at ease with the more delicate balance of Art Deco. Louis Majorelle in particular, whose *forte* had been in the sensual sculpting of organic forms, produced transitional pieces of ungainly ponderousness.

Art Deco was for the most part a feminine style expressing a characteristically French image of luxury and refinement. The style found perhaps its most satisfactory expression in the light elegance of seat furniture, in the furnishings of salon or boudoir. In the area of cabinet furniture, heaviness was a potential hazard to which many of the less talented designers fell victim. It required the sense of proportion of a designer such as Ruhlmann to achieve a pleasing balance in the mass and the support of cabinet or commode.

An important ingredient of this pursuit of refinement was the exploitation of exotic materials: rich woods, novel veneers or inlays and the luxury of the lustrous lacquers which enjoyed so strong a revival in the twenties. The dark stripes of Macassar ebony were very much in vogue, as were

Below Chambre de Dame created by Maurice Dufrêne in Art Deco style for La Maîtrise in 1925.

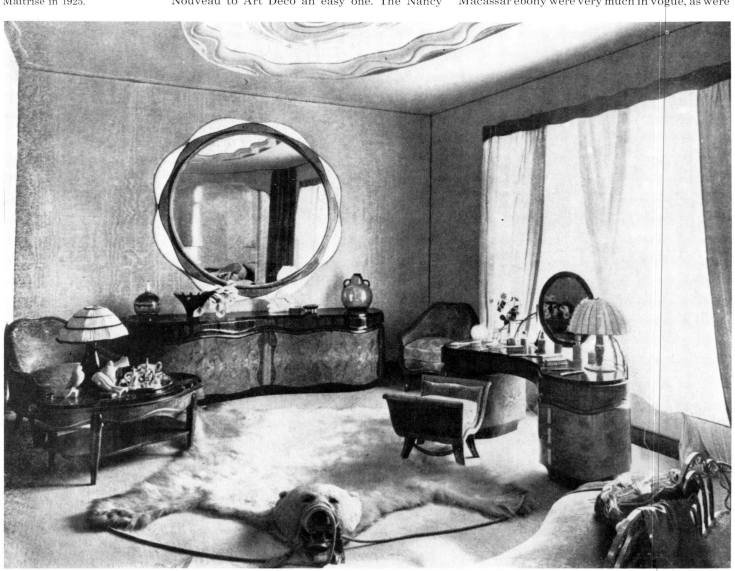

the intricate grain patterns of amboyna and walnut. Cabinet fronts and desk-tops were covered in tortoiseshell or snakeskin. *Galuchat,* or sharkskin, first used in the eighteenth century on small decorative items, was now used to give an unusual surface either to details or to the entire body of a piece of furniture. Tooled and painted leatherwork, inlays of ivory or mother-of-pearl, the various textures and types of lacquer and, later in the twenties, the use of vellum were just a part of the gamut of luxurious effects exploited by the Art Deco furniture makers.

The transitional phase was notable for the designs of Follot and Dufrêne, of Francis Jourdain, whose fresh, rectilinear style seemed to show the influence of the Wiener Werkstätte, of Léon Jallot, Henri Rapin and Bellery Desfontaines.

It was notable above all for the dramatic influence on fashion and decor of the Ballets Russes of Diaghilev. Bakst's rich designs saw the final demise of the decadent pastel subtleties of the *fin de siècle* and ushered in vibrant new colours, no less decadent, the taste for opulence and a rich confusion of patterns and motifs.

Above Dining room designed by Jules Leleu with carpets by Da Silva Bruhns, 1920s. Leleu was a cabinet-maker whose work was of a remarkably high standard of execution. As a designer, however, he lacked the flair of his peer, Ruhlmann.

Left *Chaise longue,* in two parts, designed by Maurice Dufrêne for his Chambre de Dame of 1925. Dufrêne was a talented, commercial designer who made a graceful transition from Art Nouveau to Art Deco.

Ruhlmann

The first significant group-showing of contemporary work by the leading creative furniture designers after the war years was the 1923 Union Centrale exhibition. Restricted to individual pieces of furniture rather than complete room settings, this provided a small-scale dry-run for the major international showing two years later. The 1925 exhibition was the official consecration of what is still the last great total expression of French style, comparable in its unity to the great styles of the eighteenth century. The official pavilions, decorated by the foremost cabinet-makers and artisans were the greatest monuments to Art Deco and no single designer proved his talent to greater effect that Emile-Jacques Ruhlmann, arguably the most important furniture designer and *ébéniste* of the twentieth century and a noble inheritor of the traditions of J.H. Riesener and Martin Carlin.

Ruhlmann's first exhibit was in the Salon d'Automne of 1910 and over the next ten years he was to evolve the features of his distinctive style. Pierre Patout, writing the catalogue introduction to the 1934 posthumous retrospective of Ruhlmann's work, singled out key pieces in this evolution, including a *meuble d'appui* of 1913, raised on 'delicious tapering legs', which he described as a revelation, and his *meuble au char* of

1919 in which 'the choice of wood, the scale of the ivory inlay, the interior to which a painstaking concern had brought an absolute refinement made of this piece . . . the perfect expression of his art.' A *meuble d'encoignure* of 1916 illustrated in this catalogue is a seminal design in the evolution of Art Deco by virtue of its truly spectacular exploitation of the floral theme inlaid in ivory, its decorative exuberance disciplined within a neat oval. Ruhlmann's increasing virtuosity with fine decorative inlays and veneers was demonstrated in a superb cabinet of 1920, the entire surface of which was veneered in *loupe d'amboine* inlaid with a decoration of interlooping circular lines of ivory.

After the First World War Ruhlmann had founded the Etablissements Ruhlmann et Laurent and started the commercial manufacture of his designs, though always still to the highest possible standards. He sketched and explored endless variations on his basic forms and motifs, and managed to achieve an ideal balance between elegance and refinement and the massiveness which he evidently relished. Many of his sketches were published in the folio 'Croquis de Ruhlmann' which provided a source book to a generation of less sensitive plagiarists. After Ruhlmann's death in 1933 his *ateliers* continued to work to his old designs under his nephew J. Porteneuve.

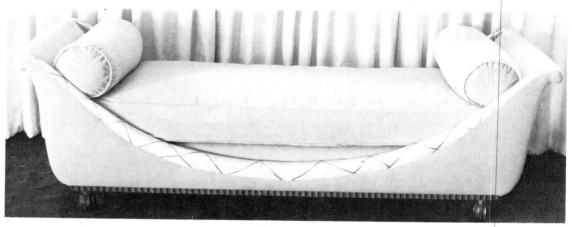

Ruhlmann

In his series of room designs for the 1925 exhibition Ruhlmann was able to express himself in the grand manner. Invited to design furnishings for the Pavillon d'un Ambassadeur, he ably demonstrated his unique blend of the monumental and the simple, the imposing understatement of discreetly rich materials and prodigious labour. His salon in the Pavillon d'un Collectionneur is an overwhelming, over-scaled expression of Ruhlmann's grand style for public rooms, the effect emphasized by the giant scale of the floral wallpaper and the imposing life-size neo-classical nudes of Jean Dupas. Ruhlmann's creations are perhaps best appreciated in isolation, for their delights are born of the combination of his eye for harmonious proportions and his consummate attention to detail. His

talent as an *ensemblier* can be seen in the perfection of his designs for door-handles or fireplaces, light fittings or frames. In the last years of his career, in such projects as his furnishings for the study of the palace of the Maharajah of Indore, he explored the language of Modernism, while never compromising his own standards of élitist hand-craft, and used chromium-plated metal as a more modish trimming than his formerly-favoured ivory.

The closest rival for Ruhlmann's title as foremost *ébéniste* in France was probably the team of Louis Süe and André Mare who collaborated in the Compagnie des Arts Français, founded by them in 1919. Their style, quite different from that of Ruhlmann, but equally distinctive and showing the same respect for tradition, was a more bulbous interpretation of neo-classicism and was characterized by high-relief carved decoration, though Süe et Mare proved themselves equally masters of inlaid decoration. Indeed, their superb cabinet of 1927 inlaid with a floral bouquet in mother-of-pearl must rank as one of the masterpieces of decorative Art Deco cabinet-making. The partnership had participated with honour in the 1923 Salon and in 1925 was invited to decorate the Musée d'Art Contemporain, a project which consolidated their well-deserved reputation as leading figures in the refinement of the Art Deco style. They enlisted the support of a highly talented team which included Paul Véra, Boutet de Monvel, Richard Desvallières and André Marty and provided a complete decorating service, creating not only furniture but fabrics, fittings and decorative objects.

Right Table designed by Emile-Jacques Ruhlmann, using an elegant neo-classical tripod base, *c.*1925.

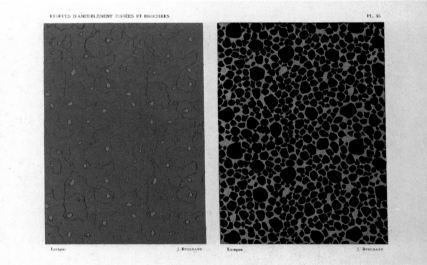

Above Fabric designs by Emile-Jacques Ruhlmann, 1920s. Ruhlmann had a prodigious concern for detail and did not restrict his activities to designing just furniture but created doors, fireplaces, light-fittings, fabrics and carpets.

Right *Meuble d'encoignure* designed by Emile-Jacques Ruhlmann in 1916. This is perhaps his most extravagant use of decorative ivory inlays in a floral design which is the epitome of Art Deco. The veneer is in his favoured Macassar ebony.

Left Inlaid cabinet by Emile-Jacques Ruhlmann, *c.*1925.

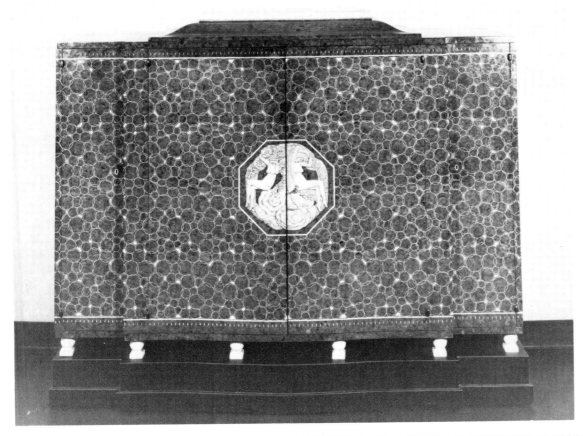

Below A spectacular and somewhat theatrical version of Art Deco in a commode by Süe et Mare. The bulbous forms are typical of their work. The colourful stylized decorations are inlaid in stained woods.

Süe et Mare/Groult

André Groult deserves individual homage, be it only on the evidence of one room, his Chambre de Madame for the 1925 Pavillon d'un Ambassadeur. A unique variant of Art Deco, this quintessentially feminine room housed a remarkable suite, the gently swollen curves of the furniture completely covered in cream sharkshin and detailed in ivory. Exhibiting from 1910 in the Salons, Groult was perhaps too strongly tied to tradition to rank as a major figure, but in this and other experiments with *galuchat* he established his niche in the story of French furniture.

Clément Mère produced furniture in a richly individualistic style. First exhibiting in 1910, he soon became known for his highly decorated version of Art Deco. He made a speciality of *repoussé* and tinted hide, carved ivory and precious wood inlays on his high luxury creations.

Left Chair and table by Süe et Mare, early 1920s.

Below left Magnificent cabinet by Süe et Mare, dating from 1927. Its spectacular bouquet is inlaid in mother-of-pearl in the dark wood.

Below *Chiffonier* in burr walnut by Süe et Mare. Made in 1923 this chest was included in the Süe et Mare exhibit at the Paris International Exhibition of 1925.

Opposite Cabinet created by André Groult for the Chambre de Madame in the Pavillon d'un Ambassadeur at the Paris International Exhibition of 1925. This is one of the most remarkable examples of Art Deco furniture design.

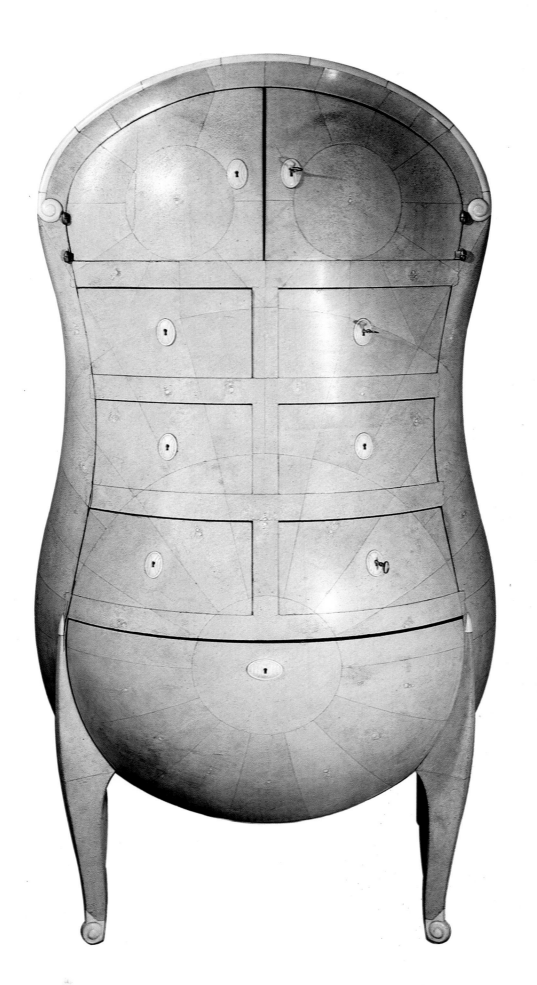

Décoration Intérieure Moderne

So many of the furniture designers of the twenties failed to emerge from the shadow of Ruhlmann's dominating influence and much of their work survives as a pale imitation of his masterful creations. Notable amongst these designers, and each capable of producing elegant furniture in the Art Deco style, are Jules Leleu, René Joubert, Philippe Petit, and the team of André Domin and Marcel Genevrière, working together from 1922 under the trade name of Dominique. Leleu first participated in the Salon des Artistes-Décorateurs in 1922, and subsequently built a reputation for his cautious but commercially successful and less sumptuous version of the Ruhlmann style. Joubert and Petit were both involved, in turn, as designers for the firm Décoration Intérieure Moderne, known as D.I.M., which had been founded shortly after the war, and like Leleu and the Dominique team, they achieved commercial success.

An influential figure in the early story of Art Deco was the *couturier* Paul Poiret who, around 1910, had transformed the colours and costumes of Léon Bakst's theatrical designs into successful fashions. As early as 1911 in the establishment of his Atelier Martine he had created a studio for decorative domestic design which was to formulate many of the motifs of Art Deco. Poiret employed talented but untrained young girls who created delightful naive floral patterns which were adapted to textiles and to the decoration of the angular painted furniture with which Poiret is particularly associated. Amongst his gifted protégés was the illustrator and designer Paul Iribe who was commissioned by *couturier* Jacques Doucet to design contemporary furniture for his Paris home. Iribe's departure for America in 1914 marked the end of this brief but fruitful phase of his career in furniture creation.

Bureau de dame, designed by D.I.M., *c.*1925. The elegant lines of this desk are covered in panels of ivory and sharkskin. The form is very similar to that of a small table designed by Rose Adler for Jacques Doucet.

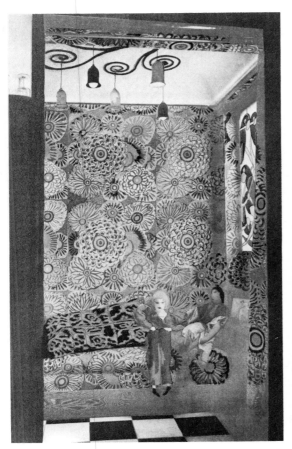

Projects for interiors by the Atelier Martine, 1924. These flamboyant schemes, which owe a good deal to the designs of Léon Bakst for the Ballets Russes are for a Telephone Room, a Landing and a Dining Room. The Atelier Martine was the brainchild of *couturier* and furniture designer Poiret.

Brandt

Above *L'Oasis*, a magnificent
wrought-metal screen
presented by Edgar Brandt at
the Paris International
Exhibition of 1925 and a
perfect example of his craft.

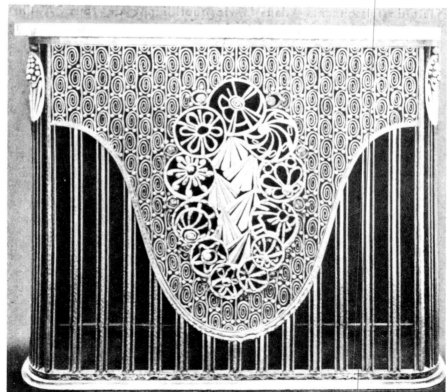

Right Wrought-iron radiator
cover by Raymond Subes,
designed in the early 1920s.

A notable feature of Art Deco was the tremendous popularity of wrought-iron furniture. The *matière* found its greatest exponent in Edgar Brandt who set up his workshops in 1919. Brandt was above all a craftsman and in the architect Louis Favier he found a designer to complete the creative team. He was a major contributor at the 1925 exhibition, with his own stand and contributions to numerous pavilions, as well as being responsible for the Porte d'Honneur. The centrepiece of his exhibit, and indeed, the masterpiece of his *oeuvre* was the spectacular five-fold screen, *L'Oasis*. Brandt was the most prominent amongst a generation of *ferroniers* which included Raymond Subes, Paul Kiss and Nics Frères. They created doors, *guéridons*, radiator grilles, mirror frames, lamp bases and *bibelots* in iron, softening the *matière* with the scrolling lightness of the decorative motifs. Brandt made a series of bronze lamps in various sizes modelled as serpents which are amongst the more theatrical extravagances of French Art Deco.

Above Wrought-iron firescreen by Edgar Brandt, 1920s. Brandt, in collaboration with Louis Favier, evolved a repertoire of Art Deco motifs appropriate to his chosen *matière* and ranks as one of the foremost craftsmen in the 1925 style.

Left Gilt-bronze serpent lamp by Edgar Brandt. Brandt included his striking and decorative serpent lamps in his exhibit in the 1925 exhibition.

Dunand

Below Cigar box and stand by Jean Dunand, 1920s. The box is richly lacquered with a decoration of a stylized stalking panther; the low table base is veneered in fine Macassar ebony.

Opposite Three lacquer screens by Jean Dunand from the 1920s. Dunand, master lacquer craftsman, employed a number of designers as well as executing his own designs. The result is the considerable variety of decorative styles in the screens and other items that bear his name.

The revival of the oriental craft of lacquer in French furniture during the twenties must be credited to the efforts of the Swiss-born craftsman Jean Dunand. Arriving in Paris just before the turn of the century, Dunand's first interest was in *dinanderie*, work in non-precious metals, and his first encounter with lacquer, just before the war, was in his exploration of techniques of patination. After the war, increasingly fascinated by this *matière*, he extended his rue Hallé workshops, setting up a furniture-making operation to provide the bases on which to apply his lacquers. Through the twenties, his most prolific and distinguished period, and indeed through the thirties, he put his name to a quite considerable range of screens, cabinets, tables, chairs and other furnishings. Among his decorative themes, many of which were the work of a group of collaborators, perhaps the most successful were strong abstract geometric motifs, sometimes showing the influence of African art, delightful *Japonisant* figures, and stylized animal subjects.

Dunand's virtuosity at his craft was perhaps best appreciated, however, in his bold use of large, flawless undecorated areas of smooth and lustrous lacquer. He made a speciality of certain techniques of decoration, giving texture in his *laque arraché* and a fascinating surface in his use of crushed eggshell inlay, creating a minute crazy-paving effect, often over entire table tops or screen panels.

His memorable contribution to the 1925 exhibition was the Smoking Room in the Pavillon d'un Ambassadeur: red-carpeted, the walls and furnishings seductively lacquered in black with African-inspired decorations and a stepped ceiling in silver lacquer. Among Dunand's many distinguished patrons was the *couturier* Madeleine Vionnet whose apartment he helped decorate in 1929 and for whom he created a remarkable games table, the four chairs tucking in to make a cube of black lacquer with a chess-board pattern inlaid in crushed eggshell. The popularity of lacquer inspired the collaboration of Dunand's skills with those of leading *ébénistes*, including Ruhlmann. Léon Jallot and Eugène Printz also used lacquer to provide a rich surface to their furniture designs.

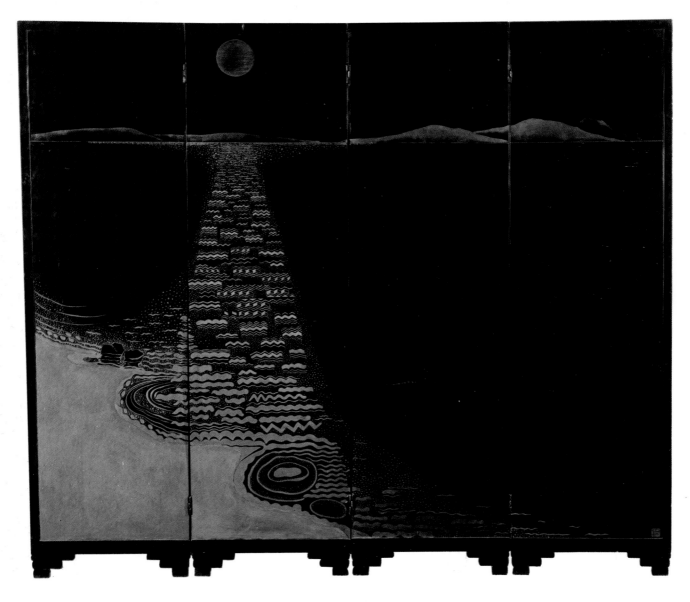

Art Deco Interiors 1

The high Art Deco style did not survive for long after its spectacular flourish of 1925. The Wall Street Crash of 1929, with its international repercussions and the emergence of the International Modernist style in the late twenties made Art Deco an indulgent anachronism. The year of the Crash was marked by the death of two of the most significant figures in the story of creative luxury French furniture of the 1920s, the *couturier* and patron of the arts Jacques Doucet and one of his most talented *protégés*, furniture designer and craftsman Pierre Legrain. These two names figure prominently in the story of what is perhaps the most intriguing facet of Art Deco, not the official and essentially traditional style of Ruhlmann or Süe et Mare which had such an appeal for the more conservative bourgeois tastes, but the exciting and novel furniture which showed the influences of

Cubism and the fashionable *art nègre* and which founds its greatest patrons in Doucet and other leading figures in the world of fashion and the arts.

Since Charles Frederick Worth had, in the nineteenth century, transformed the social standing of the *couturier* from that of a mere tradesman to that of a socially acceptable creative artist, *couturiers* had played an influential role in the French decorative arts. The work of Paul Poiret in interior decoration and in the revitalization of the art of fashion illustration is well known. Vionnet's patronage of Dunand has been mentioned. Another fruitful collaboration was the commissioning by Jeanne Lanvin of furniture designer Armand Rateau to decorate her Paris home. Working on this between 1920 and 1922 he created a delightful version of Art Deco which incorporated his distinctive furniture in a mix of archaeological styles.

Right Metal-framed laquered cabinet, designed by Eugène Printz, late twenties. Printz was one of a number of designers and cabinet-makers who enlisted the aid and skills of Jean Dunand to lacquer pieces created by them.

Opposite The Doucet villa at Neuilly: 'Le Studio du côté de la rue', 1929. Doucet's sure eye for the best of contemporary work both in the fine arts and the decorative arts made of this a remarkable interior. The desk is by Pierre Legrain.

Art Deco Interiors 2

Opposite The Doucet Villa at Neuilly: 'Un coin du studio'. The red leather armchair is by Pierre Legrain, the ebony and sharkskin table by Rose Adler.

Below The Doucet Villa at Neuilly: the Salon. The sofa is by Marcel Coard; the laquer table in front of it by Eileen Gray. The African-inspired stool in the background is the design of Pierre Legrain.

There was, however, no patron more intuitive nor more inspirational than the energetic Doucet. Until 1912 he had channelled his energies into the collecting of fine French furniture and works of art of the eighteenth century. In that year, however, he made a complete break with the past. He disposed of his collection of antiques and turned his attention to the talent around him. His first foray into contemporary decoration resulted in the commissioning of Paul Iribe to furnish his home. These first tentative essays in contemporary decoration were in a cautious Art Deco style, but Doucet's increasing familiarity with the avant-garde in painting and his new-found fascination with primitive and especially African arts were to make their mark, in turn, on the creative furniture designers whom he employed and helped develop. In 1914, with Iribe's departure for the States, his erstwhile collaborator Pierre Legrain came to Doucet's attention, and was employed by him from 1917 to make book bindings. After the war Legrain started to design furniture for Doucet and from 1926 was one of the most prominent talents involved in the furbishing of Doucet's new villa at Neuilly. His collaborators included Rose Adler, Marcel Coard,

Eileen Gray, André Groult, Clément Rousseau and Gustave Miklos. On its completion the Neuilly villa became a remarkable shrine to contemporary art and decoration, and, sadly, to the man who had brought together and inspired so many of their elements. In May 1930 the prestigious journal *L'Illustration* payed its respects with a colour coverage of the villa's spectacular rooms and an article by André Jouvin described Doucet as among the '. . . plus illustres amateurs de notre temps.'

For Doucet, Clément Rousseau made refined pieces of furniture in fine woods, ivory and sharkskin; Rose Adler's contribution included a remarkable ebony table with stepped legs, flaring sides and a sharkskin top in abstract geometric design; Coard made a *pièce de résistance*, a wide canapé carved in palisander to imitate basketwork, and trimmed in ivory. In commissions for Doucet and a handful of equally open-minded patrons Coard proved his ability to concoct a strong modern style with rich materials in sometimes unusual juxtaposition and reflecting the vogue for primitive art. Looking back in 1973, shortly before his death, on that creative decade, he lamented the rarity of such patrons.

Legrain

Above Pierre Legrain, photographed by d'Ora.

Both Pierre Legrain and Eileen Gray, despite their relatively limited production, a limitation imposed on them by the inevitable narrowness of the avant-garde market, deserve special attention as perhaps the most remarkable and innovative talents of the richly creative Art Deco period.

Pierre Legrain was the furniture designer most strongly influenced by the avant-garde fascination with African art, an influence doubtless encouraged by his acquaintanceship with Doucet, and it was for Doucet that he created his most specifically African pieces. These included a remarkable series of stools based on central African originals. One, inspired by the ritualistic stools of the Ashanti, had a scooped seat covered in sharkskin, raised on one central sharkskin-covered and four black-lacquered legs. Another stool of similar silhouette was veneered in ebony

and inlaid in mother-of-pearl, whilst another in ebony, limed and stained oak and gold leaf was inspired by a Mangbetu marriage stool. Legrain was an inventive experimenter in the use of novel materials, often in unusual contrasts and achieved surprising results with palmwood and vellum, zebra-patterned velvet and lacquer, glistening chromium-plated metal, gold or silver leaf.

Legrain found another important patron in the milliner Mme Jeanne Tachard for whom he decorated a villa outside Paris in the early twenties. Other patrons included Pierre Meyer, for whom he decorated an apartment on the avenue Matignon and the Vicomte de Noailles for whom he decorated a bedroom. Legrain's style is confident and virile and he achieves a perfect balance in his combinations of simple, often aggressive forms derived from African art and Cubism.

Opposite Armchair designed by Pierre Legrain, veneered in burr maple and with panels of tinted sharkskin, 1920s.

Right Corner shelves in gilt and lacquered wood designed by Pierre Legrain. The aggressive zig-zags are inspired by African carvings.

Below Pair of seats and low table in silvered and lacquered wood designed by Pierre Legrain for the milliner Mme Tachard. A combination of fine materials and futuristic shapes from one of the most inventive designers of the twenties.

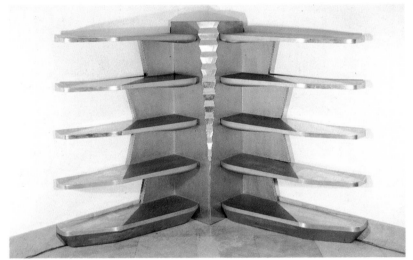

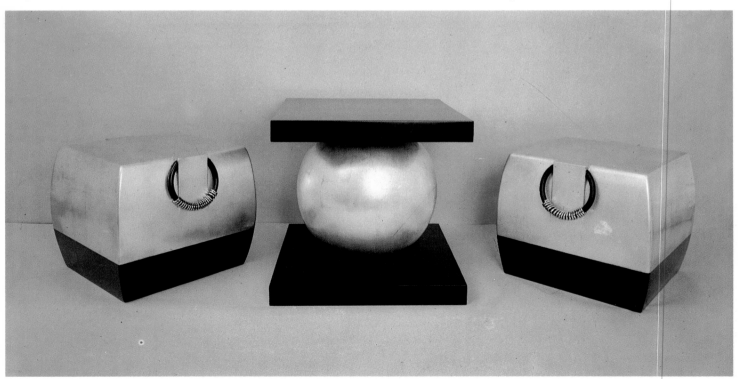

Above Bench seat in carved ebony and stained oak with gilt seat, designed by Pierre Legrain for Jacques Doucet. One of Legrain's most specifically African-inspired designs, this bench seat is derived from a traditional Mangbetu marriage stool.

Below left Desk in ebony and sharkskin designed by Pierre Legrain for Jacques Doucet. Luxurious materials and a confident, uncluttered line make this an aristocratic piece of furniture, well worthy of the great patron for whom it was conceived. Early 1920s.

Below Pierre Legrain's designs for the Doucet desk.

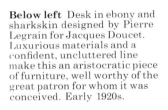

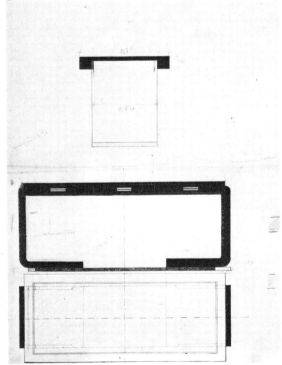

Eileen Gray

Eileen Gray is a fascinating figure. A shy but energetic Irishwoman, after completing her studies at London's Slade School, she took the adventurous step of moving alone to Paris. In 1907 she settled in the rue Bonaparte apartment which she was to occupy until her death in 1976. Her first, chance interest was lacquer, a material in which she had experimented several years before the First World War, developing an ability which was soon to attract Doucet's attention. In 1914 she completed her first major commission for the *couturier*, the spectacular four-panel screen *Le Destin*. She was to make several other pieces for him, including at least two tables, one in deep green lacquer, raised on legs carved as lotus flowers, the other a more architectural design in black lacquer with legs constructed of small blocks reminiscent of building bricks.

Miss Gray's most significant schemes in the period of her involvement with the more luxurious aspects of decoration were the apartment for Mme Mathieu Lévy on which she worked from 1919 until 1922 and her bedroom-boudoir project for the 1923 Salon des Artistes-Décorateurs. In both of these schemes, despite such decorative fantasies as the superb canoe-shaped lacquered day-bed for Mme Lévy or the futuristic lacquered floor lamp for the Salon, the significant elements were the architectural, simple folding screens of painted or lacquered rectangles and, in the Salon project, the austerity of surface decoration. Although Miss Gray was to continue her activities in the field of luxury decoration through her rue du Faubourg-St-Honoré gallery, Jean Désert, until 1930, her interests were already leading her towards the evolution of a personal version of the International Modern style. The twenties saw the brief success of several other female artists in luxury decoration,

Above right Day-bed in rough textured lacquer created by Eileen Gray for Mme Mathieu Lévy. The luxury of this piece of furniture and the extravagance of its very concept is in marked contrast to the functionalist ideals which were to inspire the second, Modernist phase of Eileen Gray's designs.

Right 'Bedroom-boudoir for Monte Carlo' presented by Eileen Gray in the 1923 Salon des Artistes-Décorateurs. The relative austerity of this decorative scheme was ahead of its time and was criticized in the press. It was, however, much admired by J.J.P. Oud of the De Stijl group, whose work was to influence Eileen Gray's own Modernist style.

Opposite top Lacquer screen by Eileen Gray. The richness of the *matière* associates this screen with the designer's luxury phase; the rigidly geometric design, however, marks the progression towards a Modernist ethic.

Opposite *Le Destin*, a lacquer screen by Eileen Gray, 1914. This richly decorative screen was Miss Gray's first important commission from the *couturier* Jacques Doucet.

among them Eyre de Lanux and Evelyn Wyld. Eyre de Lanux also worked in lacquer and described her work as 'simple extravagance.' Her strong, geometric decorations have their source in American Indian art.

Art Deco, which had developed in the early years of the century and flowered in the early twenties, was a phase in decorative design inextricably linked with traditions of luxury and almost inevitably superseded in the late twenties by the prominence of the new functionalist principles, clean lines and undecorated surfaces of Modernism. An interesting decorator who elegantly straddled the threshold was Jean-Michel Frank who used a warm mix of natural, sometimes exotic materials but always in designs and settings of the utmost simplicity. Few decorators, however, made the transition easily. Eileen Gray was a notable exception, but for the most part the thirties belonged to new names.

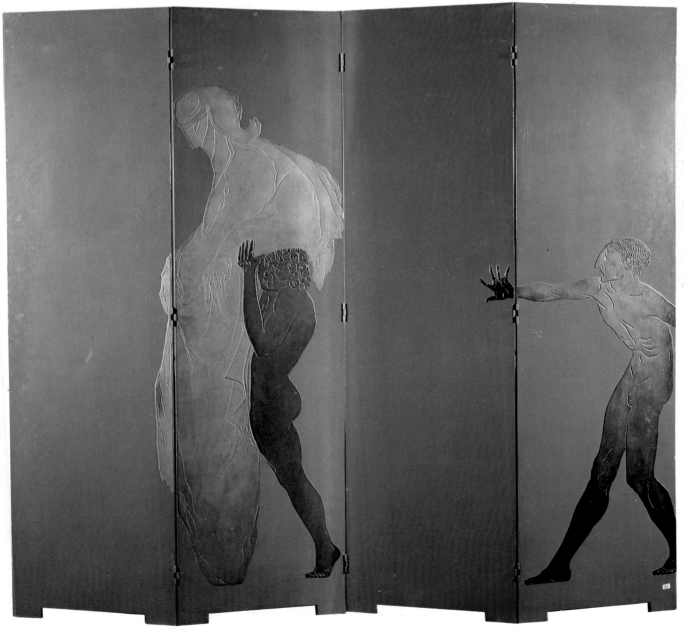

The Twenties
International Modernism

International Modernism, developing from principles first put forward in the nineteenth century and from the practical and ideological experiments of a varied, international group of precursors active around the turn of the century and during the years leading up to the First World War, emerged finally in the mid to late twenties as the most vital, the most revolutionary force ever in the evolution of furniture design. That Ruhlmann and Mies van der Rohe could have been contemporaries in itself seems extraordinary, so drastic were the innovations of the latter, so radically new the whole school of thought of which he has become perhaps the most widely recognized figurehead.

The source of International Modernism goes back to the formulation, largely by British theorists, of an aesthetic based on functionalism and the rationalization of design to the exigencies of machine production. Dr Christopher Dresser was a key figure in both the formulation and the exploration of these theories and his holloware, for example, is the obvious precursor of the formalized functionalism of Bauhaus designer Marianne Brandt's celebrated teapot.

In furniture design the obvious precursors of Modernism have been mentioned – their work ranges in style from the mannered, spatial eloquence of Mackintosh or the opulent geometry of Hoffmann and Moser to the disciplined functionalism of Wagner, Loos or the mature Behrens. Modernism had its most direct precursors in the Deutscher Werkbund and the Weimar Kunstgewerbeschule which, re-opened in 1919 as the Bauhaus, became the focal point of the movement.

The German pavilion at the
Barcelona Exhibition of 1929,
designed and furnished by
Mies van der Rohe – a supreme
expression of understated
Modernist grandeur.

Below Gerrit Rietveld with his workshop assistants and G.A. van der Groeneken (behind G.R.).

Opposite above Painted wood cabinet designed by Gerrit Rietveld in 1919. The interplay of verticals and horizontals makes this a sculptural as much as a functional design.

Opposite below left Gerrit Rietveld's celebrated 'Red–Blue' chair of 1917–18. This chair is more a statement of faith than a practical seat and expresses in three dimensions a sculptural resolution of the formal concern of the De Stijl group of artists and designers.

Opposite below right 'Zig-zag' chair designed by Gerrit Rietveld in 1936. This design, while eminently practical as a dining chair, suggests neither comfort nor stability in its angular appearance.

There emerged simultaneously a Modernist school of furniture design in the Netherlands which took its name, 'De Stijl', from the magazine published by Theo van Doesburg from 1917 until 1931. The artists and designers involved formed a fluid, loose-knit group and their collective style found its most refined painterly expression in the disciplined, contemplative canvases of Piet Mondrian, its most interesting sculptural expression in the furniture of architect Gerrit Rietveld. The De Stijl style was formal in the extreme and the same rigid principles were applied as much to painting as to furniture design. One commentator on the group aptly illustrated a Mondrian composition opposite a room from the seventeenth-century Imperial Katsura Palace at Kyoto. Both are made up of carefully counterbalanced rectangles, outlined and contained by rigidly disciplined verticals and horizontals. Several commentators have emphasized this Japanese quality of austerity and sophistication in the work of Rietveld whose furniture became a three-dimensional exploration of the formal problems which Mondrian, van Doesburg and Bart van der Leck sought to resolve on canvas.

Rietveld's ideology differed from that of the Bauhaus in that function remained secondary to the resolution of formal, spatial problems. He himself admitted, 'A practical realisation was not always feasible. Function for me was a thing by itself which I never overlooked, it is true, but it did not come into play until the construction and spatial exercises in De Stijl had been completed . . . The fact that I am constantly concerned with this extraordinary idea of the awakening of consciousness, may account for my work being inevitably oriented towards spatial problems.' Comparing his own achievement with that of the Bauhaus he concluded, 'The Bauhaus approach was very dif-ferent in that it attempted to develop form on the basis of a clear definition of the function. Having a strong sense of relativity, I did not think that function as a point of departure was a sound approach. Function was an accidental, casual need that would change with the time and indeed always changes in the course of time.'

Rietveld trained from the age of eleven as a cabinet-maker in his father's workshops and set himself up independently in 1911. From 1908 dates his first unornamented design of strict horizontal/vertical construction, a plain and severe armchair. Between 1911 and 1915 Rietveld took evening classes in architecture under P.J. Klaarhamer and in 1915 made up a series of pieces of furniture to his designs in a rigid and simple Arts and Crafts style.

In most of his own furniture designs Rietveld concealed the wood, painting it in the strictly limited palette of the De Stijl aesthetic – black, white, red, blue and yellow. The De Stijl furniture aesthetic found its most perfect, most controversial expression in Rietveld's remarkable 'Red-Blue' chair of 1917-18, by any standards a landmark in the story of furniture design. Rietveld wrote of it in later years that '. . . made of two boards and a number of laths, that chair was made to the end of showing that a thing of beauty, a spatial object, could be made of nothing but straight, machined materials.'

Van Doesburg and fellow De Stijl architect J.J.P. Oud designed furniture in a more rational vein, both exploiting tubular steel in the twenties and making contact internationally with other progressive designers, while Dutch functionalist architect Mart Stam claims the credit for having designed the first cantilever tubular steel chair in 1926, preceding similar Bauhaus designs.

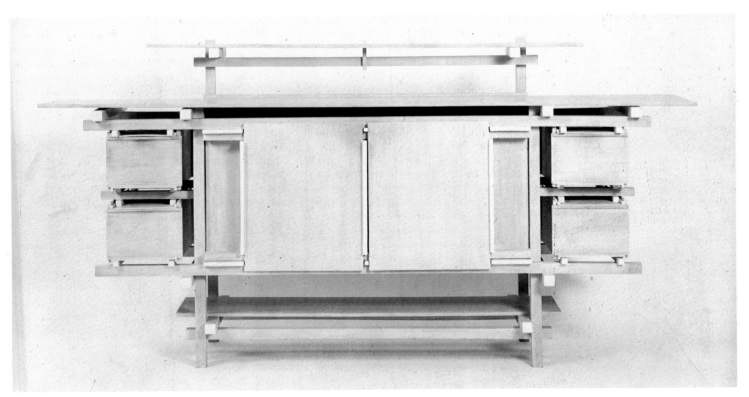

Germany **Bauhaus**

Below The Bauhaus building at Dessau.

Bottom Members of the faculty of the Dessau Bauhaus photographed together in 1926. They are, from left to right: Josef Albers, Hinnerk Scheper, Georg Muche, Laszlo Moholy-Nagy, Herbert Bayer, Joost Schmidt, Walter Gropius, Marcel Breuer, Wassily Kandinsky, Paul Klee, Lyonel Feininger, Gunta Stölzl and Oskar Schlemmer.

Opposite The Amhorn House project at Weimar, 1923.

Stam's achievement, and indeed the whole De Stijl effort, was to be greatly overshadowed, however, by the exceptional expressions of Modernism nurtured in the progressive atmosphere of the Bauhaus. Gropius, confirmed as director in 1919, became a vociferous advocate of a dramatic new approach to design and in his writings conveyed the idealism and the dynamism of the Bauhaus ethic, an ethic which brought together painter, sculptor, architect, designer and craftsman in a co-operative atmosphere.

In his manifesto of April 1919 Gropius wrote, 'The complete building is the final aim of the visual arts. Their noblest function was once the decoration of buildings. Today they exist in isolation, from which they can be rescued only through the conscious co-operative effort of all craftsmen. Architects, painters and sculptors must recognize anew the complete character of a building as an entity. Only then will their work be imbued with the architectonic spirit which it has lost as "salon art" . . . Let us create a new guild of craftsmen, without the class distinctions which raise an arrogant barrier between craftsman and artist. Together let us conceive and create the new building of the future, which will embrace architecture and sculpture and painting in one unity and which will rise one day toward heaven from the hands of a million workers. . . .'

Gropius's lofty idealism was practical rather than romantic and elsewhere he had expressed his realization that '. . . an architect cannot hope to realize his ideas unless he can influence the industry of his country sufficiently for a new school of design to arise as a result.' It was an aim of which, despite a long saga of administrative and political difficulties which were to haunt the Bauhaus until its final closure by the authorities in 1933, Gropius and his colleagues could justly claim the achievement. In furniture design the Bauhaus revolution was in the creation of models in metal appropriate for series production.

Bauhaus/Breuer 1

Most prominent in the early exploitation of metal for furniture was the designer Marcel Breuer who, having joined the Bauhaus as a student in 1920, became a master in 1925 at the time of the move from Weimar to Dessau, where he took over the carpentry workshop, restyled, appropriately, in 1925 as the furniture workshop, when the emphasis shifted from wood to metal. Gropius had himself taken charge of the carpentry workshop for three previous years and, before him, Johannes Itten had been form master. Nineteen twenty-five marked a major turning point in the story of modern furniture.

Writing in 1928, Breuer attempted to explain his motivation in turning to metal, 'Metal furniture is part of a modern room. It is styleless, for it is expected not to express any particular styling beyond its purpose and the construction necessary therefore. The new living space should not be a self-portrait of the architect, nor should it immediately convey the individual personality of its occupant . . . The furniture . . . is broken up airily, sketched into the room as it were; it impedes neither movement, nor the view through the room. . . . I purposely chose metal for this furniture in order to achieve the characteristics of modern space elements just described. The heavy, imposing stuffing of a comfortable chair has been replaced by a tightly fitted fabric and some light, springy pipe brackets. The steel used, and particularly the aluminium, are remarkably light, though they withstand severe static strain. The light shape increases the flexibility. All types are constructed from the same standardized, elementary parts which may be taken apart or exchanged at any time. This metal furniture is intended to be nothing but a necessary apparatus for contemporary life.'

Breuer succeeded in implementing his ideal of impersonal, visually light and spacious furniture, creating a wide range of designs between 1925 and his departure from the Bauhaus in 1928. These were put into production by the Berlin firm Standard-Möbel and by the firm of Thonet who willingly made the natural transition from bentwood into tubular steel, though never abandoning the manufacture of the bentwood on which the firm's reputation had been built.

Breuer's first exercise in tubular steel, however, was far from the styleless, impersonal functiona-

Right Armchair designed in 1924 by Marcel Breuer and constructed in oak with wool upholstery. An angular design which bears comparison with the work of the De Stijl group.

lism which he advocated. Designed in 1925 for the Dessau campus home of his colleague Wassily Kandinsky and named after the painter, the 'Wassily' chair was in fact a highly symbolic and highly complex design, as much a sculptural exercise and a statement of faith as a machine for sitting in and, in its exploration of spatial values, the direct descendant of Rietveld's 'Red-Blue' chair. Like the 'Red-Blue' chair, the 'Wassily' was a complex arrangement of flat planes, in this case canvas or hide seat, back and arms, and of straight structural elements which intersected and over-lapped one another as the wood elements of Rietveld's chair had done.

More in keeping with Breuer's avowed functionalist minimalism were designs such as those used in the much-illustrated *haus piscator* in Berlin of 1926, the standardized, co-ordinated ranges of austerely simple seat and table designs for Standard-Möbel, several of which are still in production today, as are his 'Wassily' and the cantilever design which he first introduced in 1928. Breuer devised a prophetic scheme for modular storage units, functional versatile and thoroughly modern.

Left Nesting tables designed by Marcel Breuer in tubular metal. The tops are of lacquered wood in this set made for the French designer Robert Mallet-Stevens.

Below The 'Wassily' chair designed by Marçel Breuer in 1925 and named after his Bauhaus colleague, Wassily Kandinsky, for whose campus home the design was conceived. This complex chair in tubular steel and canvas or hide has the distinction of being the first use of tubular metal in furniture and the idea is credited to Breuer's chance observation on the qualities of tubular steel in providing lightness and solidity in the construction of bicycles.

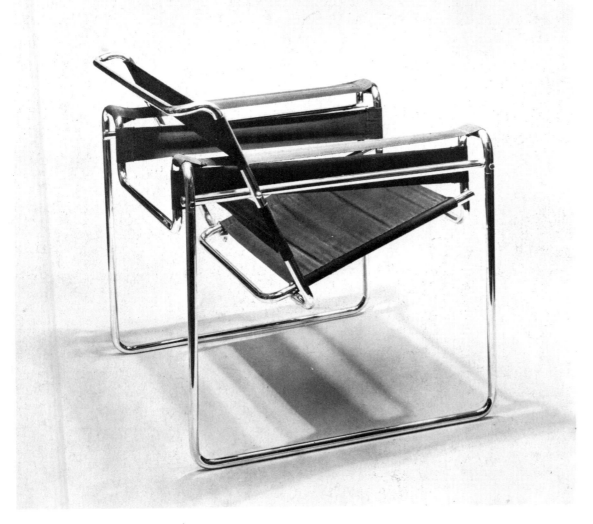

Bauhaus/Breuer 2

Right The interior of the *haus piscator*, furnished sparsely by Marcel Breuer in a style that could be regarded with equal justification as clinically cold and uninviting or elegantly minimal, 1926.

Below right 'Moholy' dining room in the Dessau master houses, with chairs, table and sideboard designed by Marcel Breuer, 1926.

Above Cantilever chair designed by Marcel Breuer in 1928 in tubular steel. Breuer's design has earned a lasting popularity and is still manufactured in large quantities. It cannot, however, claim the distinction of being the first tubular metal cantilever chair, an honour which goes to an earlier design by the Dutchman, Mart Stam.

Other designers at the Bauhaus used both wood and metal in pursuit of the same austere aesthetic. Among Gropius's most satisfying designs was his *étagère* of 1923 in cherry wood and mirror-glass, a simple, functional construction of five rectangular shelves and eight upright dividers, but at the same time a finely-tuned counterbalance of solids and voids, mass and line, evoking the imperial Japanese interior which had made such an appropriate counterpoint to a Mondrian composition. The point that emerges is, of course, that despite all protestations of stylelessness, the foremost designers at the Bauhaus were in fact masterful stylists who embraced a functionalist, machine aesthetic, but appreciated nonetheless the profoundly cerebral stylistic potential of the strict disciplines which they willingly imposed upon themselves.

Another prominent Bauhaus designer concerned as much with sculptural as practical considerations was Josef Albers. He designed chairs which could be easily dismantled for packing and transport, both in bentwood and in metal. He had betrayed his concerns for the sculptural aspects of furniture, however, in earlier projects such as his wooden shelf unit and table designs of 1923, in both of which intersecting planes create relationships of solid and void which evoke the formal preoccupations of the De Stijl group, above all those expressed in the Rietveld chairs.

Above Armchair designed by Josef Albers. Designed in 1928 in wood, this chair can be easily dismantled for ease of transport and storage.

Left Interior of the Gropius master house at the Bauhaus.

Bauhaus/Mies van der Rohe 1

Right Ideas for chairs sketched by Mies van der Rohe in the thirties. Van der Rohe devised a small number of basic ideas for chairs and explored countless possibilities of variants which, for the most part, were never made up even as prototypes.

Below Side chair designed by Mies van der Rohe for the Weissenhof Housing Exhibition held in Stuttgart in 1927. The illustration is taken from the publication *Innenräume*.

Perhaps the most sophisticated exponent of the austere Bauhaus style, although in fact a relative late-comer to the school, was architect Mies van der Rohe, probably the most uncompromising purist of Modernism and acknowledged by the majority of critics as the most important and most influential architect, not merely of the Bauhaus, but of the entire Modern Movement. He accepted the post of director at the Bauhaus in 1930 after the brief interregnum of Hannes Meyer, Gropius's successor. Mies had known Gropius since their meeting during their apprenticeship in the Berlin office of Peter Behrens in the years following the foundation of the Werkbund. Mies ran his own architectural office in Berlin from 1919 and had in fact already formulated his concepts of furniture design and conceived several of his most important designs before his 1930 appointment.

The first assertion of Mies's genius as a furniture designer came in 1927 with his tubular steel designs exhibited in schemes created in collaboration with Lilly Reich for the Werkbund Exhibition, Weissenhofsiedlung, at Stuttgart, and for the silk exhibit at the Exposition de la Mode in Berlin. Mies unveiled his own version of the steel cantilever chair, admittedly not the first chair to use the structural principle, but certainly the first chair to carry the principle through to its full potential exploitation. For where Stam had used rigid curves in the design

of his cantilevers. Mies drew his chair frame in an elegant sweep which exploited the intrinsic flexibility of the material. 'I was', he wrote, 'the first to have exploited consistently the spring quality of steel tubes. I made the experiments in early summer of 1927 and applied for a patent on August 24 1927.' A stool and coffee table followed the chair.

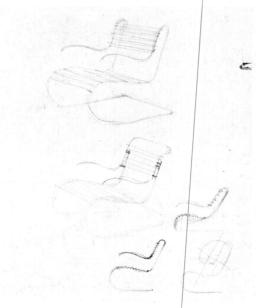

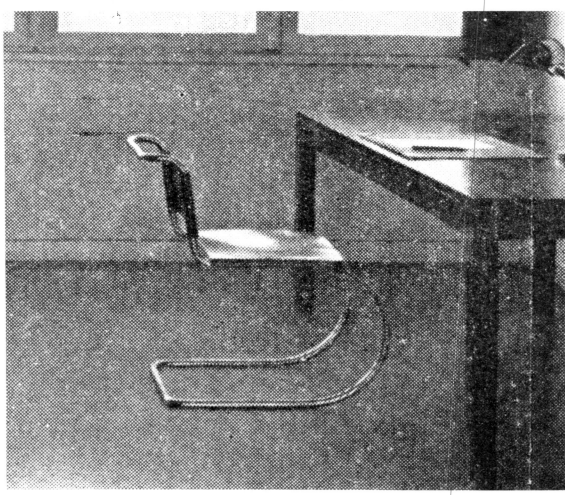

Above Bedroom furnishings included in the Berlin Building Exhibition in 1931. The tubular steel framed chair is by Mies van der Rohe, the tubular steel bed and table by Lilly Reich.

Left The 'Barcelona' chair designed by Mies van der Rohe for the German pavilion at the Barcelona International Exhibition in 1929. The framework is of flat steel, the cushions of hide – the supreme statement of Mies' approach to furniture design. 'God', he maintained 'is in the details', and the details, as indeed the overall proportions and concept of this classic design, cannot be faulted.

Bauhaus/Mies van der Rohe 2

It was in his furnishings for the German pavilion at the 1929 Barcelona International Exposition, however, that Mies was to achieve the consummate expression of his Modernist style, at once uncompromising and luxurious, aristocratic and austere. Invited to design the national pavilion as the setting for an inaugural ceremony conducted by the King of Spain, Mies devised a scheme which, while small in scale, was truly regal in character, incorporating a pair of his celebrated Barcelona chairs as thrones.

For these chairs, and the ottomans and tables designed *en suíte* he used flat steel, a material which demanded hand finishing and which had a more substantial, a more imposing presence than tubular steel. The seat cushions were of meticulously seamed and buttoned hide. Rich hide, seamed in the same strict grid, was used by Mies in conjunction with walnut and tubular steel in his sublime and truly patrician couch of 1930. In these designs, in the various designs for the Tugendhat house project undertaken in 1929 and in the numerous variations of his basic themes, Mies van der Rohe demonstrated an unfailing eye for detail and a perfect sense of harmonious proportions. 'God,' he said, 'is in the details.'

Interior of the Tugendhat House at Brno, designed in 1930 by Mies van der Rohe and incorporating his side chairs in tubular steel and black lacquered cane and the 'Brno' chair, one of a range taking their name from the project.

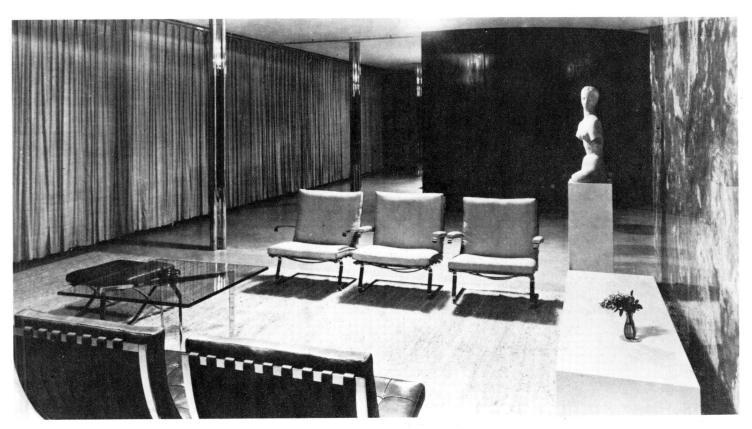

Above Sitting area within the
Tugendhat House, Brno, 1930.

Left 'Brno' armchair designed
by Mies van der Rohe, 1930.
This is the flat steel version of
a design which was also
executed in tubular steel.

France Le Corbusier

If Modernism found its most forceful expression in Germany and, in particular, within the Bauhaus, it was by no means without its advocates in other countries. The Dutch made a significant contribution, but the major contribution outside Germany came from a loose-knit group of architects and designers in Paris, many of whom, after first working independently, came together in 1930 in the Union des Artistes Modernes. Prominent amongst them, and an untiring idealist and spokesman for Modernism was Swiss-born architect, Le Corbusier (Charles-Edouard Jeanneret).

Modernism emerged slightly later in France than in Germany or the Netherlands, in spite of Le Corbusier's definition as early as 1921 of the home as '. . . a machine for living in' and the Modernist ethic expounded by Le Corbusier and others in the twenty-eight issues of the journal *L'Esprit Nouveau* published between 1920 and 1925. The French furniture industry of the early twenties was deeply conservative and, despite the superficial novelties of the Art Deco style, fundamental attitudes had hardly changed since the eighteenth century. Fine materials, meticulous craft and fashionable, rather than truly modern, design were the ruling factors. In his study of 1925, *L'Art décoratif d'aujourd'hui*, Le Corbusier illustrated

strictly functional metal office furniture as a worthy basis for a new furniture aesthetic: 'These designs are cold and brutal, but they are appropriate and honest – these are the right criteria.'

Amidst the luxury and decorative refinements of the 1925 Paris International Exhibition, Le Corbusier's simple and Modernistic contribution, the Pavillon de L'Esprit Nouveau, pointed the way to the future development of progressive French furniture design. The pavilion was more interesting as a spatial, architectural exercise than for its furnishings, however. Although Le Corbusier devised plain metal cabinet furniture for the interior, he used standard Thonet bentwood chairs and was not to design his own classic Modernist seat furniture until, three years later, he undertook the furnishing of a villa in Ville d'Avray. For this project, working in collaboration with Charlotte Perriand, he conceived three seats which are acknowledged masterpieces of the Modern Movement.

The most remarkable of these was the 'Chaise Longue', the concept and construction of which were entirely without precedent. The seat frame, contoured to the lines of the body and raised on two arcs, was in tubular steel with steel webbing and a loose seat cover upholstered in fabric or hide to

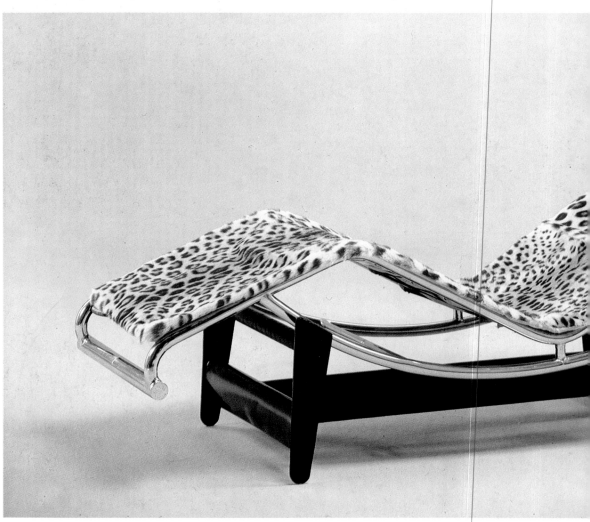

support the sitter. This upper unit rested on the rubber-covered stretchers of the steel base and was adjustable for position. Charlotte Perriand illustrated the 'Chaise Longue' in an extraordinary statement of faith published in 1929 in *The Studio* which she opened with the declaration, 'Metal plays the same part in furniture as cement has done in architecture. IT IS A REVOLUTION.'

The two other chairs which were the fruit of their collaboration were the 'Basculant' and the 'Grand Confort'. The former, taking its name from the pivoting back rest, was a noble but, by 1928, hardly a revolutionary essay in tubular steel. The concept of the 'Grand Confort' was more remarkable, for

this chair literally turned inside out the traditional design of the deep-upholstered chair, the cushions being contained within the cradle framework rather than serving to conceal it.

The 1925 Exhibition gave an opportunity also to the architect Robert Mallet-Stevens to demonstrate his faith in the Modernist aesthetic in his design for the Pavillon du Tourisme. In his interiors Mallet-Stevens stripped away superficial decoration, filled his rooms with light and a sense of space. He designed metal furniture in the new idiom though adding a personal touch by painting the metal in bright colour. In 1930 he became a founder member of the U.A.M.

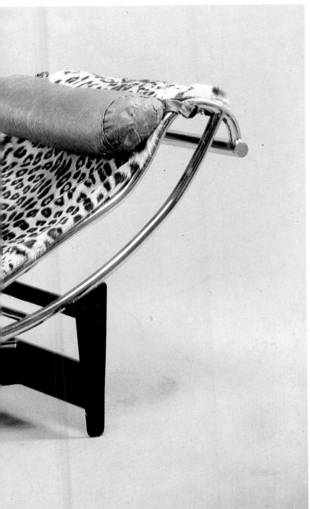

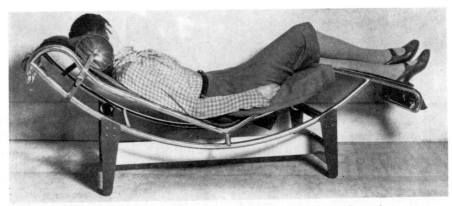

Metal Couch designed by Le Corbusier, Pierre Jeanneret and Charlotte Perriand

WOOD OR METAL?

Union Des Artistes Modernes

Another significant contributor to the 1925 Exhibition was Pierre Chareau, though his exhibit, the Bureau-Bibliothèque pour l'Ambassade Française, was a cautious compromise between Modernism and Art Deco. Chareau enjoyed using rich materials and never sacrificed his taste for quality in the pursuit of functionalist design honesty. As early as 1924 he had produced the first of a remarkable series of desks with wrought flat iron band frameworks and pivoted trays. Chareau's *chef d'oeuvre* of domestic architecture and furnishing was the 'Maison de Verre' built and fitted out between 1928 and 1931 for Dr and Mme Jean Dalsace. Within the visually spacious structure, defined by walls of glass bricks and by exposed steel columns, Chareau set his metal furniture; in the reception rooms the flooring was of off-white studded rubber which, even today, half a century later, would seem dramatically modern.

Nineteen-thirty saw the consecration of the French Modern Movement in the foundation of the U.A.M., with Hélène Henry, René Herbst, Francis Jourdain, Robert Mallet-Stevens and Raymond Templier as founder committee members. Senior amongst them was Jourdain who had sought to avoid the trap of ornamentation in furniture design in the years before the First World War. Looking back, as honorary president of the U.A.M. after its first twenty-five years of activity, he defined the fundamental error made by Art Nouveau designers, the error of according too much importance to ornamental and decorative considerations.

In the regular exhibitions which they were to hold from 1930 the U.A.M. group showed their concern for practical above decorative considerations. In 1949 they inaugurated their first aptly-named 'Formes Utiles' exhibition. The materials used by the U.A.M. designers were the materials first promoted by the Bauhaus with the emphasis, inevitably, on metal and glass, the symbolic materials of the Modern Movement. The most talented of the French Modernists, however, treated these materials with a distinctive flair and created unusual and stylish designs, in many cases with the potential for series production, but often dictated by a pursuit of style, elegance and even luxury in a modern guise.

Foremost as furniture designers amongst the members of the U.A.M. were René Herbst, Louis Sognot, Mallet-Stevens, Chareau, Gray and Perriand. Amongst the most impressive projects undertaken by Herbst were the furnishings designed in 1930 for S.A. the Princess Aga Khan, a commission which gave him the opportunity to be excitingly modern without any compromise of quality. Louis Sognot found a major patron in the young Maharaja of Indore, for whom, in collaboration with Charlotte Alix, he designed spectacular furnishings. The Maharaja's palace became a shrine to the Modernist fashion, just as the Maison de Verre had been a shrine to the doctrine.

Above Desk and stool designed by Pierre Chareau and made in flat iron with wooden tops and seat. One of a number of variants on this idea developed by Chareau through the twenties from its initial inception c.1924.

Right 'Chaise Longue' designed by René Herbst in 1930 in tubular steel. The back is adjustable for angle. Herbst was a leading figure in the propagation of Modernism in France as an influential founder member of the Union des Artistes Modernes.

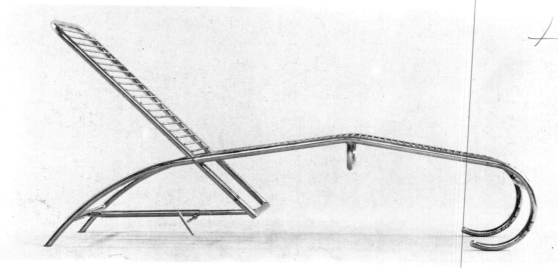

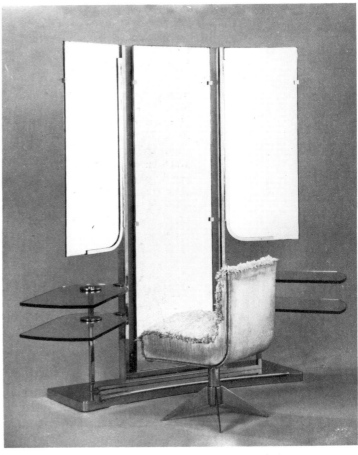

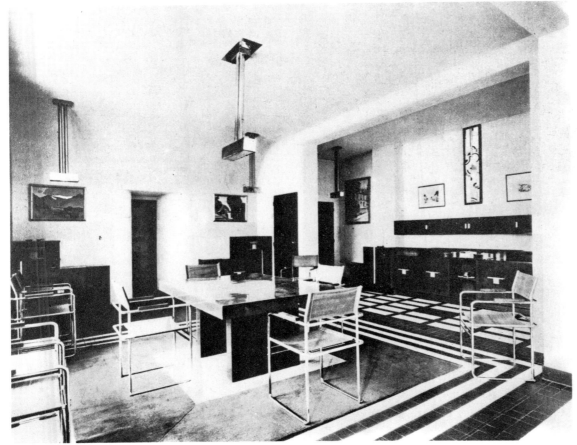

Above left Interior scheme by Djo-Bourgeois, a stylish decorator in the Modernist style, 1929–30.

Above Dressing table designed by Louis Sognot in collaboration with Charlotte Alix in chromium-plated metal and aluminium and with swivelling glass side tables. c.1931–3. Sognot was a stylish exponent of a chic French version of Modernism.

Left Dining room designed by Robert Mallet-Stevens, c.1930.

Eileen Gray

Right Screen built up of panels of black lacquered wood, designed by Eileen Gray. This idea was first developed by Eileen Gray in the decoration of the apartment of Mme Mathieu Lévy, completed in 1922. A small number of versions exist in varying sizes.

Below 'Transat' armchair designed by Eileen Gray in 1927 in lacquered wood, chromium-plated metal and leather. An elegant design marking a transition from the designer's earlier fascination with the luxury of lacquer and her development towards a stylish functionalism.

Below right Tall screen in strip metal and sheet celluloid. The crescent section panels fold into one another and two handles allow the folded screen to be easily carried. This screen was designed by Miss Gray for her own rue Bonaparte apartment where it remained from the time of its creation *c.*1930 until her death in 1976.

Eileen Gray was one of the most consistently inventive designers of the French Modernist school. Her initial impetus had come in the early twenties when her encounters with the teachings of the De Stijl group crystallized her instinctive search for a modern aesthetic. She paid homage to the De Stijl influence in a remarkable sculptural table designed in 1922, a two-colour construction of intersecting vertical and horizontal planes. Eileen Gray used perforated metal, tubular steel, sheet celluloid and a variety of other materials in a series of prototype designs, few of which were put into production, but which reflect her fertile and genuinely modern attitude to furniture design after the abandonment of her initial love, lacquer.

Around 1930 Modernism had moved on from being the idealistic dream of a relatively small number of pioneers to become a fashionable style of decoration. Herbert Hoffmann's seminal 1930 study of International Modern Interiors shows just how quickly and how far the language of Modernism had spread. The thirties were to see the expansion of Modernism in the hands of purists who further explored the potential applications of Modernist theory in furniture design and of designers and decorators who found in it an attractive new stylistic vernacular.

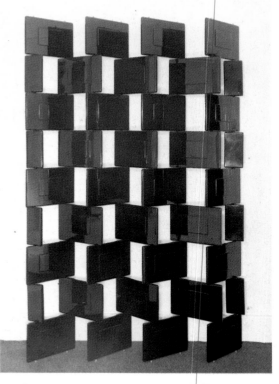

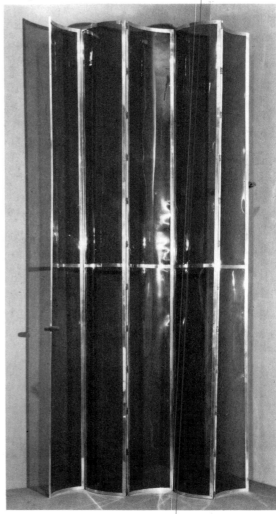

Table in painted wood
designed in 1922 by Eileen
Gray. Made in the first year of
her contract with the De Stijl
group, this table is a sculptural
homage to their influence.

The Thirties
Modernism and Eclecticism

Furniture design in the thirties presents a rich diversity. It was a decade of eclecticism which explored many styles and ideas and saw the creation of furniture which ranged from the austerely functional to the indulgently romantic or the Surrealist.

The decade opened with the fashion for Modernist furniture at its peak. Steel and glass and the rejection of decoration were very much in vogue. By the close of the decade, however, a general reaction had set in against the wilfully bare look and the purely decorative was once again prized as the pendulum of taste made its seemingly inevitable swing.

Modernism did not die, by any means, but it certainly evolved from the idealism which had characterized its inception. It became as much a decorator's style as a theorist's and the ingredients of Modernism were incorporated into a luxurious and stylish mode of decoration. Purists, meanwhile, maintained the traditions of the founders of the movement. Mies van der Rohe continued to add to the catalogue of his sophisticated designs. Alvar Aalto in Finland evolved a fresh Scandinavian-style Modernism. In the United States, on the other hand, Modernism was taken as a basis for a new approach to furniture design with style as the goal. The results have contributed to an image of American design in the thirties which has earned for the decade the label 'The Streamlined Decade'.

For many designers, however, and certainly for a large proportion of a fickle public, Modernism as a fashion had soon had its day and was overtaken by essentially romantic styles with more than a glance towards the past. The neo-baroque, or neo-classical styles which found increasing popularity from the early thirties made welcome allusions to tradition and to notions of comfort and opulence.

In France, meanwhile, the early thirties saw the development of International Modernism as a decorator's style. The ideological background was obscured by the pursuit of chic as an end in itself. The resulting interiors were often of considerable elegance and sophistication, if at times somewhat inhuman and theatrical.

A most interesting demonstration of the transition from the more decorative aspects of the twenties to the new bareness so fashionable at the turn of the decade can be seen in the redecoration of the Paris apartment of Mme Mathieu Lévy. This had been decorated in the early twenties by Eileen Gray in a dark, rich vein. Redecorated by Paul Ruaud, the apartment was featured in 1933 in an article in *L'Illustration*. Here, in place of decorated lacquer panelling, were bare surfaces, white walls, glass flooring and white block screens in place of the former black lacquer. Light and space became key elements in a scheme which sparkled with chic. The furniture created for the original apartment by Eileen Gray took on a new character, a character emphasized by the addition of later Modernist designs by Miss Gray and completed by carefully placed zebra skins.

One designer-decorator who has not yet received the critical attention which his work merits is Djo Bourgeois, an artist of the interior whose elegant restraint achieved a Japanese sense of purity and whose schemes were characterized by delicate ice-cream colours.

Through the thirties, the designers of the Union des Artistes Modernes (U.A.M.) explored every conceivable variant on the visual language of Modernist furniture, at times merely following in the path of Bauhaus precursors, at other times, however, creating interesting precursors of post-war styles.

Tubular steel and glass were of course very much in evidence, but there was also an increasing use of wood, not in meticulous cabinet-work but, rather in the manner of Aalto, in furniture of simple design adaptable to series production. The post-war vogue for rattan was also beginning.

Opposite Room designed by Frank Lloyd Wright for the Kaufmann Department Store, Pittsburgh, 1937. The strictly rectilinear concerns of the first generation of Modernist designers were modified during the 1930s in the United States to produce stylish and luxurious interiors.

Below The Paris apartment of Mme Mathieu Lévy, redecorated in a Modernist style by Paul Ruaud, with furniture by Eileen Gray, who had by this time entered a Modernist phase in her designs.

Below Design for an interior by French designer, Djo-Bourgeois, in a modulated Modernist style, *c.* 1930.

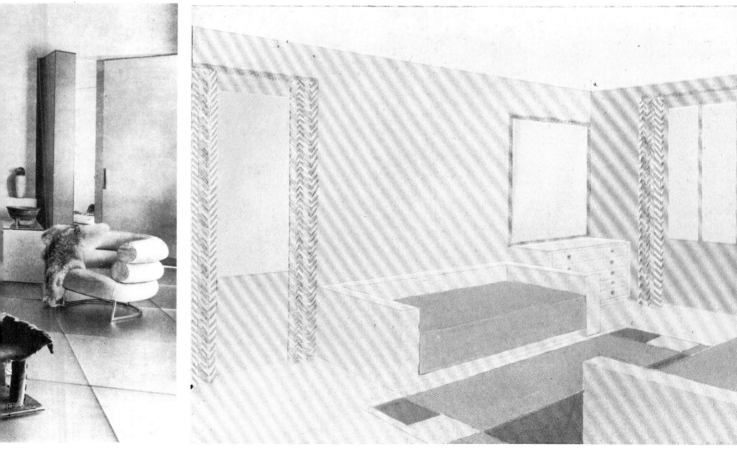

Thirties Modernism/the Indore Palace 1

Right One of a pair of standard lamps designed for the Maharajah of Indore by Eckart Muthesius *c.*1930–3 with a base in painted wood and the main column in alpaca and panels of white glass.

Below Low cabinet designed by Muthesius for the Indore palace, in alpaca and lined with light wood, with glass sliding doors, *c.*1930–3.

Perhaps the most remarkable decorative scheme in which the artists of the U.A.M. were involved was the decoration between 1931 and 1933 of the palace of the Maharaja of Indore. This spectacular project was supervised by the young Eckart Muthesius, son of Hermann Muthesius, who had played so influential a role in establishing the concepts of modern domestic and industrial design in pre-First World War Germany. Muthesius designed many of the furnishings for the palace himself and enlisted the collaboration of leading designers, craftsmen and manufacturers in the Modernist style from France, England and Germany. Notable amongst his own contributions were the various lamps and light fittings, the metal tables and cabinets and a remarkable pair of library chairs. From England came various Pel designs including seating specially upholstered in red leather or with red-painted seats and backs. From Germany came chairs by Zeffner and Luckardt.

From France, in addition to classic designs, which included Eileen Gray's 'Transat' chair and Le Corbusier's 'Chaise Longue', came specially commissioned furnishings by Emile-Jacques Ruhlmann, in his less characteristic Modernist vein, and Louis Sognot in partnership with Charlotte Alix, as well as designs by René Herbst and carpets by Da Silva Bruhns. Sognot created remarkable beds, in aluminium for the Maharaja, in chromium-plated metal and glass for the Maharani, a chic Modernist version of the traditional games table and various other designs. The Indore schemes were supremely stylish in a hard and uncompromising, though luxurious vein.

Thirties Modernism/the Indore Palace 1

Left Games table and four armchairs designed for the Maharajah of Indore by Louis Sognot and Charlotte Alix, *c.*1930–3; the frames are in chrome, while the arms, backs and seats of the chairs are in synthetic material.

Below This desk for the Maharajah in Macassar ebony and chrome by Emile-Jacques Ruhlmann shows the tendency by the designer to move towards a more Modernist approach during the early thirties. The desk is dated 1932.

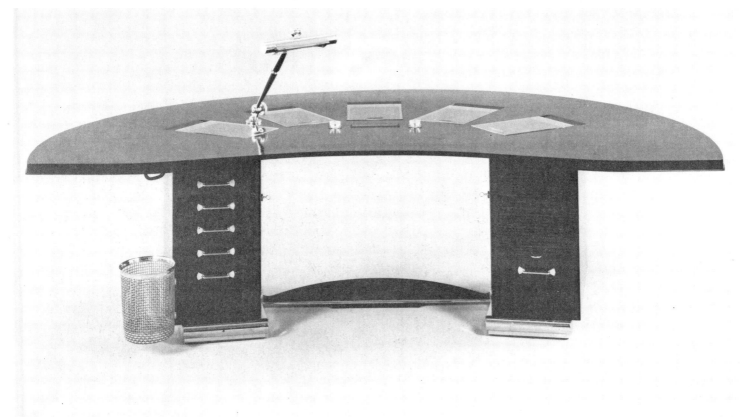

Thirties Modernism/the Indore Palace 2

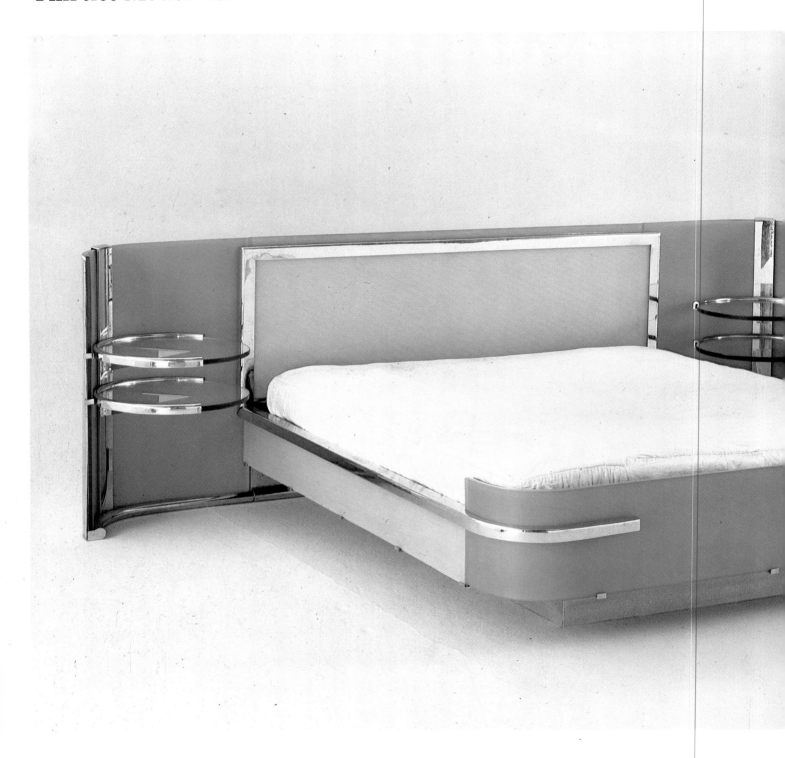

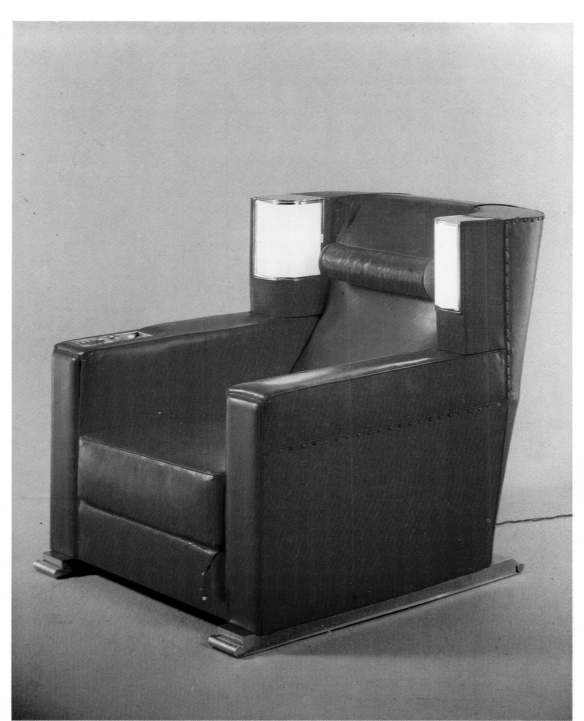

Above A glass and chrome bed designed by Louis Sognot for the bedroom of the Maharani of Indore, *c.*1930–3.

Above One of a pair of armchairs with reading lamps incorporated, designed for the palace of Indore by Eckart Muthesius, *c.*1930–3. The covering is in brilliant red synthetic material.

Surrealism and Eclecticism 1

Below The 'Mae West lips' sofa, designed by Salvador Dali in 1936 and used by Jean-Michel Frank in an interior scheme for the Baron de l'Epée.

The pared-down style which was a key feature of Modernist furniture and decoration found one of its most subtle and individual exponents in the Parisian decorator/designer Jean-Michel Frank. Not for him the coldness of steel or the harshness of white walls or emphatic angularity. Instead, he used natural materials in their natural colours, achieving subtle harmonies of creams, beiges and browns by the use of such ingredients as vellum, sharkskin, ivory, split straw, rock crystal, wool and suede. Frank's career started in the twenties and he came to prominence around the turn of the decade with such projects as his contribution to the Templeton Crocker apartment in San Francisco and his salon for the Vicomtesse de Noailles.

As the thirties progressed, however, Frank came to incorporate within his schemes more fanciful elements, the work of such collaborators as Alberto and Diego Giacometti, Christian Bérard and Salvador Dali. For *couturier* Elsa Schiaparelli he had created furnishings which were a departure from his usual restrained style and which caused Coco Chanel to shudder '. . : as if she were passing a cemetery.'

Schiaparelli wrote, 'Frank made me an enormous couch in orange leather and two low armchairs in green. The walls were white and the curtains and chair covers were made of a white rubber substance that was stiff and gleaming. The tables, like bridge tables, were black with glass tops, the wall sofa

chairs were in green rubber . . .'

Alberto and Diego Giacometti collaborated on a range of bronze furniture for Frank, loosely inspired from the antique. These included tables, chairs and lamp bases constructed of slender elements and with terminals in the shape of archaic animal or human heads. Alberto Giacometti also modelled a variety of plaster vases, *torchères* and other fittings in forms which combined surreal and archaic references.

The most memorable Surrealist furnishings of the thirties, which provided so salutary a change from the ultimately stifling self-consciousness of Modernism, were the work of that master of the unexpected, Salvador Dali. Most celebrated of his creations is the sofa upholstered in red fabric and designed in the form of a pair of voluptuous lips, supposedly those of Mae West. The 'lips' sofa was conceived in 1936 and was used in Jean-Michel Frank's scheme for a ballroom/projection room for the Baron de l'Epée and in the English home of Edward James, an important patron of Surrealism.

Another of Dali's whims was a chair with the back supports ending in hands, carved in full relief, and raised as if in supplication. The Paris Surrealist exhibition of 1938 encouraged inventive and disturbing ideas for furniture. One of the most publicized exhibits was a stool by Kurt Seligman, 'L'ultra-meuble', supported on legs and feet carved, quite literally, as human limbs.

Below Bronze chair designed by Alberto and Diego Giacometti for Jean-Michel Frank, mid-thirties. The Giacomettis also designed bronze tables for Frank.

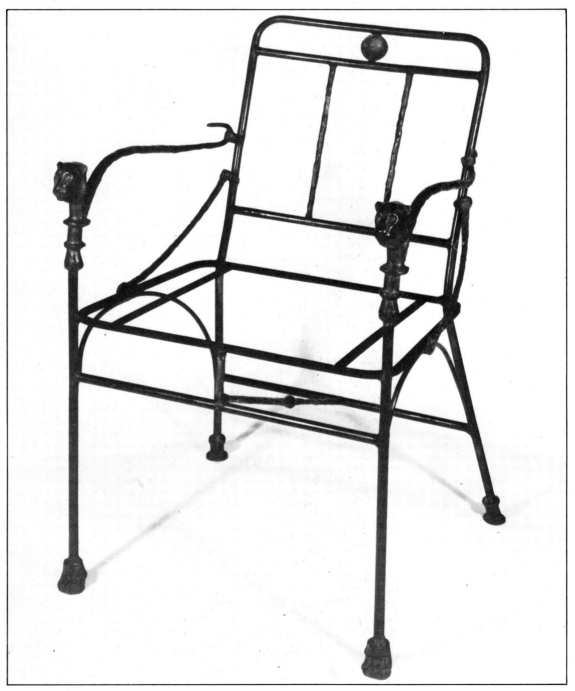

Surrealism and Eclecticism 2

Surrealism was a minority indulgence. It was, nonetheless, a fad in furniture design which was indicative of a more generalized search for new directions. The thirties saw the development of the fashion for antique styles as an inevitable reaction to Modernism. Cabinet-makers entered a new phase of historicism, with only a minority making furniture in a simple, modern vein. Decorators used antiques with a new enthusiasm, laying the foundations for today's commonly accepted practice of using antiques of various styles and eras often in clever and startling juxtaposition.

A key name in this evolution of the decorator's style is that of Carlos de Bestegui. When Modernism was the very height of fashion, de Bestegui had commissioned Le Corbusier to create an apartment in Paris in the most austerely modern style. By the time the architectural schemes were completed, however, their startling bareness, the plain walls, plate-glass windows and simple, uncluttered spaces no longer made the novel impact which de Bestegui had anticipated. The Modernist style seemed somehow *passé* in avant-garde circles and so he reacted by using Le Corbusier's architecture as a setting for the most extravagantly indulgent decorations, incorporating opulent seating, dripping chandeliers and a remarkable over-scaled blackamoor specially made for him in Dresden.

De Bestegui's neo-baroque whims were a timely

Above and left The roof garden and drawing room of the Paris apartment of Carlos de Bestegui, designed in an especially austere Modernist style by Le Corbusier and then, in reaction to its stark lines, furnished by its owner in a highly eclectic manner.

if extreme response to a renewed desire for decorative fantasy in furniture and furnishings which was to characterize the thirties. During this decade, French cabinet-makers developed a not-always-satisfactory eclecticism. Ruhlmann's death in 1933 marked the close of an era of disciplined style, the advent of a somewhat uneasy historicism. Louis Süe, who, with André Mare, had been so stylish and pure an exponent of Art Deco, was responsible in the late thirties for one of the most indulgent exercises in thirties decorative fantasy in the furnishing of the Paris apartment of Mme Helena Rubinstein. Mme Rubinstein's magpie collection of antique furniture and antique and modern works of art was housed by Süe in settings of baroque splendour. One memorable feature of the schemes, and destined to become a characteristic decorative element of the era was the padded, quilted satin which Süe used in the bedroom, covering doors and entire walls.

This phase in decoration saw the creation of relatively little furniture of real merit. Many decorators preferred to use antiques, sometimes repainted or modified to suit a decor, choosing them for effect rather than historic interest. One of the more interesting of the French furniture designers of this decade was André Arbus. His exhibits at the Paris Exhibition of 1937 were an elegant distillation of his style, characterized by neo-classical features.

Above and left Interiors in the Paris house of Helena Rubinstein, designed by Louis Süe, c.1938. Modern and African art and a varied collection of antiques were displayed among furniture by Jean-Michel Frank.

Below and opposite below Laminated wood and plywood *chaise longue*, designed in 1936 by Marcel Breuer for Isokon, later made in an upholstered version; this was perhaps the most effective design to come out of the liaison between the masters of the Bauhaus and English furniture manufacturers during the thirties.

Opposite above Marcel Breuer's design for an Isokon chair in plywood, 1936.

The Modernist style did not find real acceptance in the United Kingdom until the beginning of the thirties. Britain's furniture designers had muddled through the twenties without distinction. Only a few, notably Gordon Russell and Ambrose Heal, made a cautious attempt to come to grips with the modern style.

In the period from 1928 to the mid thirties, however, a more lively group of designers, more in tune with international developments, broke new ground, promoting a sleek and stylish Modernism. Foremost amongst them was Russian-born Serge Chermayeff, who married into the conservative decorating firm of Waring and Gillow in 1928 and immediately transformed its image, introducing a number of progressive designs in December of the same year.

Another tentative move in the direction of International Modernism had been the invitation extended in 1929 by Jack Pritchard to Le Corbusier to design an exhibition at Olympia for the firm of which he was at that time a manager, Venesta. In 1931 Pritchard, Chermayeff and the architect Wells Coates travelled to Dessau to study at first hand the work of the Bauhaus. They returned to England more convinced than ever of the validity of the Bauhaus approach to design and determined to implement the style and the ideology in Britain.

Modernism became an exciting and revolutionary phase in British furniture design under the influence of this group and their like-minded contemporaries, just as the movement was losing force in Germany.

Marcel Breuer and Walter Gropius both moved from the increasingly restrictive climate of Germany to participate for a few years in the promotion of Modernism in Britain. Breuer worked in Britain between 1935 and 1937. Gropius had left Germany in 1934, sponsored in his move to Britain by Jack Pritchard. By 1937, however, in which year

both he and Breuer left to assume teaching posts in the United States, the British public had tasted and for the most part rejected the uncompromising character of Modernist furniture and design.

During their brief spell in England, Breuer and Gropius contributed a number of furniture designs to the progressive firm of Isokon, founded in 1931 by Jack and Molly Pritchard, Graham Maw, Robert Spicer and Wells Coates. Jack Pritchard and Wells Coates, though not directors of the firm, were its shaping force and it was they who introduced the Bauhaus émigrés to design furniture.

Breuer's best known designs for Isokon are his laminated wood and plywood *chaise longue* of 1936, and his nest of tables in birch ply designed in February of 1936. Gropius also designed furniture in plywood around the same date, both designers finding, perhaps, a compromise between the hardline approach of the Bauhaus and British traditionalism by using wood in preference to metal.

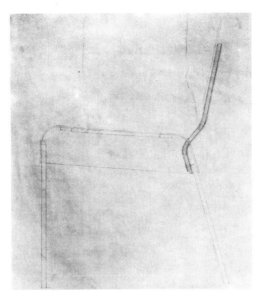

United Kingdom **Modernism 2**

Below Armchair in bent plywood, designed by Gerald Summers and manufactured by Simple Furniture Ltd., London, c.1934.

Gerald Summers was responsible for a series of inventive applications of plywood for the explicitly named firm 'The Makers of Simple Furniture'. Bauhaus styles of tubular steel furniture were copied and developed into a quite extensive range by the firm of Pel. The initials stood for Practical Equipment Limited, a company registered in 1931 as a subsidiary of the Birmingham-based firm of Accles and Pollock. A London showroom was opened in December 1931 and very soon Pel furniture was in strong demand. The 1932 catalogue maintained that 'Steel furniture is not a novelty but an inspiration of efficiency which originated about thirty years ago, through its hygienic and structural satisfaction of medical requirements.' It was reported in 1935 that the market for tubular steel was '. . . steadily growing . . . Steel furniture is fast ceasing to be the concern of a few "ultra-moderns," and is being taken up by all sections of the community.' Pel furniture was used by the B.B.C. in their prestigious new Broadcasting House and found its way into stores, hotels and restaurants as a symbol of modernity.

The Modernist style found several interesting individual exponents in the thirties in Britain. Notable among them was the designer-decorator Oliver Hill who made daring use of glass and Denham Maclaren who designed stylish furniture, most memorably a glass, marble and tubular metal table of considerable beauty. Perhaps Hill's most distinguished achievement in glass was the exhibit designed in 1933 for Pilkington Bros at the Dorland House Exhibition. Here he showed clear glass furniture, a dressing table, stool and *chaise longue* in a setting of glass walls and floor tiles.

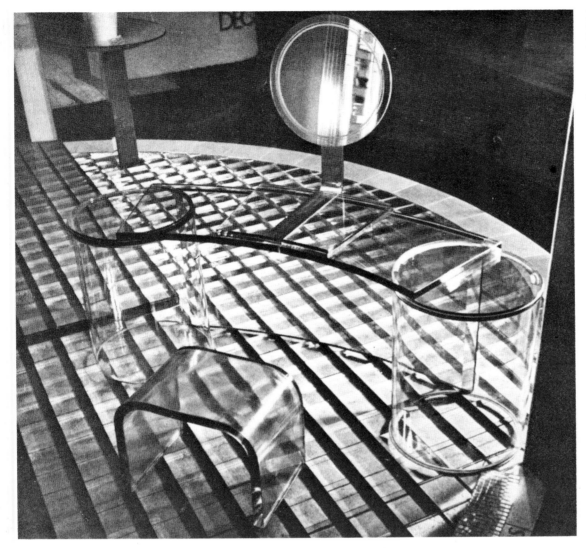

Left A dressing table in glass designed by Oliver Hill in 1933 for Pilkington Bros and shown at the Dorland House Exhibition.

Below left and right Tubular steel chair and table by Pel (Practical Equipment Limited), *c.*1931, showing that the influence of the Bauhaus had begun to spread to England by the early years of the decade.

United Kingdom **Eclecticism**

The trends which characterized French furniture design in the thirties can be seen also in the story of British design, though the British did not indulge with such unbridled panache in neo-baroque fantasy. There was in Britain the same reaction to austerity. Designer/decorator Alistair Maynard and decorator Syrie Maugham were leaders in this reaction. Maynard, who established his Grosvenor Street practice in 1935, introduced a variety of deliberately non-functional features in furniture made up to his design by the firm of Betty Joel Ltd. These included the use of decorative fluting, a feature taken up by a number of designers and used in details such as pedestal bases or over the entire surface of cabinet furniture. Maynard was one of several designers to indulge in the luxury of quilted satin for beds and seat furniture. Betty Joel, the Knightsbridge based designer/decorator, was herself responsible for stylish furniture.

Syrie Maugham is perhaps best known for the furnishings of her own elegant drawing room, a symphony in mirror-glass and off-white, from the early thirties. As the decade progressed, however, in the words of Martin Battersby, 'Mrs Maugham's interiors tended to become more and more filled with decorative furniture and ornaments which were charming and fantastic but which were really superfluous. . . .'

The most lasting image of British furniture in the thirties, however, is surely the image of large-scaled dining and bedroom suites veneered in high-polished figured woods. Vast dining tables with sets of tub-backed chairs, heavy sideboards and, of course, the ubiquitous cocktail cabinet epitomize the era. Indeed, the cocktail cabinets, lined in mirror-glass or sycamore, capture the flavour of the thirties more than any other item of furniture.

Below A music room designed by Vanessa Bell and Duncan Grant, and exhibited at Alex Reid and Lefèvre Limited in 1933.

Opposite below Typical British interior of the 1930s, incorporating large-scale furniture in highly polished wood and tub-backed chairs.

Left Interior and furniture designed by Betty Joel, early thirties.

Below left Folding glass screen designed by Syrie Maugham, early thirties.

Below right Cecil Beaton's portrait of his sister in Syrie Maugham's celebrated off-white drawing room of 1933; the setting is distinctly Modernist, incorporating long settees and a tall screen of very narrow panels of mirror.

United States **Streamlined Moderne 1**

Below The women's lounge at the Radio City Music Hall, New York; a striking example of the way in which Modernist and Deco elements were combined to produce the Streamlined Moderne style of American interior.

Opposite top A late twenties Moderne bedroom, with steel furniture, designed by Norman Bel Geddes.

In the United States of America, despite the recession which followed the crash of 1929, the thirties was a remarkable decade in the story of furniture design, as in every area of design. It was the decade in which a new generation of visionary designers proposed a quite extraordinary version of Modernism. Theirs was a style built up from highly potent symbols of speed, dynamism and the aesthetic of the machine, a style which found its most expressive forms in the sleek, streamlined contours of trans-continental trains, motor cars and airplanes.

The style was created by a handful of industrial designers whose concern with packaging and styling manifested itself in their treatment of projects of every sort and on every scale, from small domestic objects to planning a city of the future. They included most notably Norman Bel Geddes, Henry Dreyfuss, Walter Dorwin Teague and Raymond Loewy.

These designers were to express the apogee of their collective style, which has been aptly dubbed 'Streamlined Moderne', in the installation of the 1939 New York World's Fair. This Fair, on the theme 'Building the World of Tomorrow', was a fitting finale to a highly expressive decade in American design, the fantasy elements of which were to be overshadowed in the forties in the area of

furniture design by the new rationalism of Eames and his contemporaries.

The first explorations of an American Modernism in furniture design were encouraged by an exhibition organized in 1929 by the Metropolitan Museum of Art, New York. The direction that design was taking was clearly evidenced in the title, 'The Architect and the Industrial Arts'. The show's exhibits were produced by important companies working closely with distinguished designers. Unlike their French counterparts, who were chiefly cabinet-makers, the American designers were mainly architects and had very different values.

The cautious Modernist innovations of the 1929 show were overshadowed by the stylish installations of the 1934 follow-up. Here, Eliel Saarinen distinguished himself with an elegant 'Room for a Lady' and the team of Raymond Loewy and Lee Simonson presented a 'Designer's Office and Studio' in which horizontal metal banding and fluid curves of tubular steel were exploited as obsessive features of a new style. Another notable exhibit was the 'Living Room' presented by William Lescaze, a room distinguished by its utter simplicity. The 1934 show was characterized by '. . . an effort to use only those materials and forms which could be reproduced economically. . . .'

Left American Moderne
furniture of the early thirties.

Above The study of a model
house, designed by Norman
Bel Geddes, 1930.

United States **Streamlined Moderne 2**

Right Radiator grill in the foyer of the Chanin Building, New York, designed by Jacques Delamarre, c.1930.

Below Furniture designed by Donald Deskey for the private suite of S.L. Rothafel ('Roxy') in the Radio City Music Hall, New York, early thirties.

Opposite Bathroom in cream and gold tiles by Jacques Delamarre in the executive suite of the Chanin Building, New York, 1929. The metal fittings are all gold-plated, emphasizing again the mixture of extravagance and simplicity which was a characteristic of American Moderne.

In addition to those designers already mentioned, the contributors to the 1934 exhibition included Archibald Manning Brown, Arthur Loomis Harmon, Walter Dorwin Teague, Gilbert Rohde, Paul Philippe Cret and Donald Deskey. Norman Bel Geddes' project for a House of Tomorrow was a significant early expression of the Streamlined Moderne style in domestic decoration.

Streamlined Moderne furniture, popular in the thirties in the domestic context, found perhaps its most appropriate setting in the furbishing of the interiors of liners, trains and planes, where the sleek lines appropriately symbolized movement. It was a style based on a fantasy vision of a world of easy travel and mechanized living uncluttered with references to the past and in itself a dream image for the future.

In the United States the Streamlined Moderne style was forced to compete through the thirties with an increasingly prevalent decorator's style which incorporated genuine antique and Baroque-modern furniture in a somewhat theatrical hotch-potch.

After the self-conscious purity of Modernism, the thirties saw the advent of furniture and decorating styles of a fascinating diversity, often highly theatrical, fanciful settings providing an element of escapism in a decade of uncertainty, clouded from the outset by the repercussions of the Crash of 1929 and destined to close with the outbreak of war.

Scandinavia **Modernism**

Right Laminated birchwood chair by Alvar Aalto, *c.*1930.

Below Alvar Aalto's own house in Helsinki, built 1934–6.

A more practical idea of Modernism was explored in Finland by architect designer Alvar Aalto, whose first, revolutionary, chair design was created for the Paimio Sanatorium project in about 1930. Aalto used wood, preferring its natural warmth and mellowness to the coldness of metal and designed a light chair with a plywood seat and laminated birch side units, arms, legs and stretchers drawn in one unbroken sweep.

It was a chair conceived for easy mass-production and Aalto established the factory facilities to manufacture this and subsequent designs under the trademark Artek. Aalto conceived further classic designs for the furnishing of the Viipuri library. Perhaps most interesting of these new designs was his cantilever chair of 1933, the first adaptation of the cantilever principle to chair design in wood as opposed to steel, the laminated birch providing precisely the right balance of flexibility and resilience.

Opposite above left Armchair with laminated bent frame and one-piece plywood seat and back, designed by Aalto, *c.*1934.

Opposite above right Stacking stools designed by Aalto for the Viipuri Library, 1929.

Opposite below Furniture designed by Alvar Aalto during the early thirties; especially notable in the development of Scandinavian furniture disign during the thirties is his 'Armchair 406' of 1933 in bent laminated wood with a webbing seat (right).

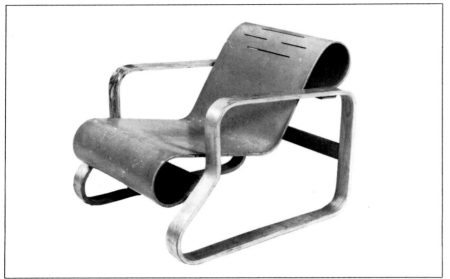

The Forties/Fifties
New Materials, New Styles

Right Cabinet by Frank Austin and Neville Ward, before 1949. The charming decoration of the door panels reflects the taste for romantic decoration in the post-war years.

Below Lounge chair designed by Charles Eames in moulded plywood and steel rod; the basic formula for this chair design was Eames's innovation and one in which he developed numerous variants. The multi-directional moulded ply and slender supportive structure are strongly characteristic of his work, *c.* 1944.

The circumstances of the Second World War, involving the shortage of materials, proved crippling to the furniture industries of Europe and it was not until after the war that the tastes for pattern in furnishing materials and for exaggerations of style were allowed free rein.

The war imposed drastic cut-backs in the furniture industry in Europe. It was left to the new generation of American designers (such as Eames, Bertoia and Saarinen) to persevere through the war years, despite certain manufacturing restrictions, with the evolution of a new, softened, less overtly dogmatic version of functionalism, turning away from the austerity of the Bauhaus look and paving the way for post-war design. In Europe, it was the British who most successfully rationalized furniture design and manufacture in a government-supervised scheme during the lean war and immediate post-war years.

Windsor *bergère* suite,
designed by Lucien Ercolani,
manufactured by Furniture
Industries Ltd, made in beech
with a waxed finish, the table
in beech and elm, *c.* 1955.

United Kingdom

The 'Utility' scheme, as the British plan for wartime furniture design was called, hardly provided the answer to the public's desire for a romantic alternative to Modernism, but it did have the very beneficial effect of bringing sound principles of design and economical and rationalized processes of manufacture to the British furniture industry.

The beginnings of the shrinkage of the industry which led to the need for the imposition of rationing and production schemes could be seen in the Control of Timber (No. 1) Order of 5 September 1939. Further restrictions on the use of timber were to follow in 1940, together with restrictions on fabrics and metals, all the raw materials of the industry. In February 1941 the British government introduced its Standard Emergency Furniture, initially intending to supervise the economic manufacture of replacement furnishings for people whose homes had been damaged by bombing. Despite the efforts of the Central Price Regulation Committee, shortages led to profiteering and 1942 saw the realization that the only way to hold down prices and rationalize production was to impose a scheme on the entire industry. On 8 July the membership was announced of the newly created Advisory Committee on Utility Furniture. This included Miss Elizabeth Denby, specialist in the planning and equipment of low-cost housing; John Gloag, consultant on industrial design; and, most significantly, Gordon Russell, whose role as design consultant was to be of central importance.

The formal introduction of Utility furniture came in November with the Domestic Furniture (Control of Manufacture and Supply (No. 2)) Order, 1942. This instituted the Utility designs, published in a catalogue early the following year, as the only designs which could legally be manufactured after January 1943 and instituted a Board of Trade licensing system for manufacturers. Gordon Russell was a great crusader in bringing intelligent design to a wide public, whether that public liked it or not. In fact he underestimated the public's desire for ornament and, writing in 1946 on the possible future benefits of the Utility programme, dreamed of a design Utopia which was never to emerge. 'I felt', he wrote, 'that to raise the whole standard of furniture for the mass of the people was not a bad war job. And it has always seemed sound to me, when in doubt as to people's

requirements, to aim at giving them something better than they might be expected to demand. Surely ...' he continued, '... it might be possible to use the Utility specification as the basis of a quality mark in the post-control period.'

The release from Utility restrictions, however, was marked by an eager return to the cosy reassurance of mixed patterns, historicism and ornament that would have destroyed the faith of all but an unswerving optimist such as Russell.

The Utility designs, soberly constructed and of sturdy, essentially rectilinear and undecorated form, were certainly an effective solution to a pressing problem, but by 1948 the trade was anxious for greater liberty and the scheme started to loosen its hold with the introduction of design freedom within the Utility programme. The Utility mark, which guaranteed a certain standard of quality, also allowed exemption from purchase tax, encouraging the trade to maintain the standards imposed through the war. The Utility furniture programme came to a close finally in 1952 with the Utility Furniture (Marketing and Supply) (Revocation) Order of that year. The British public was at last freed from war-imposed restrictions.

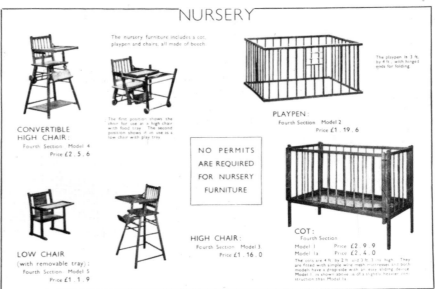

Europe

The post-war years saw a complex transitional phase in furniture design. Following the American lead, a few European designers, notably in Britain, were pioneering a new, more organic style of functionalism. From several countries came lively new trends and pleasing new directions. In Italy a loose-knit group of designers were evolving stylish new forms for furniture: inventive, innovative and refreshing. The Milan Triennale Exhibitions of 1948 and 1951 were to demonstrate the vitality of this new Italian school.

The Scandinavians, meanwhile, taking up the principles of functionalism first explored before the war, were evolving a mellow humanist version of functionalism. They favoured discreet, soft contoured forms as being more appealing than the hard lines and angles of pre-war Modernism, and exploited the warm visual and tactile appeal of natural materials. Making its mark internationally during the fifties, the Scandinavian style was to become a major shaping force of the Contemporary look and oiled Danish teak its most ubiquitous material.

Simultaneously, there emerged many distinct indications of a strongly conservative streak which, in clinging to outdated pre-war ideas, was to slow the development of furniture design. France and Germany were among the most conservative countries in this respect. Many French cabinet-makers poured their energies into the creation of obsolete and ponderous cabinet furniture which was a clumsy and unsuccessful attempt to continue the traditions of the eighteenth century, traditions for which there was no real place in the modern context. In Germany, the end of the war was marked by a strong trend towards historicism in interior decoration and a furniture industry which could so easily have become a progressive element in the revitalization of German industry was for the most part held back by the strong demand for reproduction styles.

In Great Britain, even within the work of designers ostensibly working towards the creation of new styles, there was much evidence of a search for lost roots, a strong link with tradition asserting itself as a welcome measure of stability.

Chest designed by Jacques Adnet before 1954-5 and manufactured by the Compagnie des Arts Français. The metal frame and handles are bound in hide, the front veneered in mahogany. Hide covering became very much in vogue for luxury French furniture after the war and Adnet was a prominent exponent of the technique.

Tradition and Innovation

Left Commode by Jules Leleu dated 1953, richly veneered and inlaid in mother-of-pearl; by the early fifties this type of free-standing cabinet furniture conceived along traditional lines was obsolete.

Below left Chair design by P. Pothier *c.* 1952. This French designer has taken the ingredients evolved by Charles Eames and exaggerated them in a design which seems almost a caricature of the original source.

Below Project for an aluminium and plastic chair by Clive Latimer for Heal & Sons Ltd, published in 1947.

United States

Right Dining chair designed by Charles Eames, moulded walnut ply and steel rods, 1946.

Opposite above left Coffee table designed by Irina A. Klepper *c.* 1952 and manufactured by Wor-De-Klee Inc.; the plate-glass top is supported on a substructure of light grey mahogany.

Opposite above right Table by the Italian firm Fontana Arte *c.* 1957; the plate-glass top is supported on a sculptured, free-form base in carved walnut, imitating American styles.

Opposite below Living room designed *c.*1950 by the American partnership of Kim Hoffmann and Stephen Heidrich. The centre table with its kidney-shaped glass top and base in white specially hardened plaster is a concession to the vogue for free forms in an otherwise restrained decor.

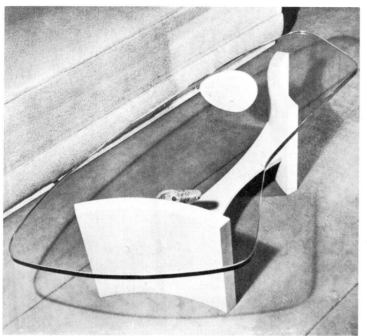

United States

The greatest innovations during the forties were to come from the United States. Despite restrictions on manufacture imposed by the war, there was no restriction on creativity in the United States.

New York's Museum of Modern Art played an important role in encouraging good furniture design with a sequence of competitions and exhibitions. The first, and probably the most significant, was the competition for 'Organic Design in Home Furnishings' held in 1940 and inspired by a suggestion from the department store, Bloomingdales, of an inter-American competition to identify the talent amongst the emergent generation of designers. The competition led to an exhibition of winning entries the following year, in which Charles Eames first came to the attention of a wide public for his remarkable designs, submitted in partnership with Eero Saarinen. In 1946 the Museum devoted a small exhibition to the 'New Furniture Designed by Charles Eames'. The following year Mies van der Rohe was invited to arrange the installation of Eames's furniture within M.O.M.A.'s exhibition 'One Hundred Useful Objects of Fine Design'. In 1948 the Museum spread its net internationally with its 'Competition for Low Cost Furniture Design', organized by Edgar Kaufmann Jr., in which British designers Robin Day and Clive Latimer distinguished themselves, winning first prize in storage furniture.

American industry contributed invaluable technological advances to the story of furniture design. Of particular significance was the development in 1941 by the Chrysler Corporation of their 'cycle-welding' technique for the binding together of wood and rubber, glass or metal. Devised in the war specifically for use in the military sector, these techniques were to open up numerous new possibilities in post-war furniture manufacture.

A significant factor in the evolution of a strong and influential mode of American furniture design was the informal American, and particularly West Coast, style of living, the 'California style', which encouraged flexibility of open-plan spaces, adaptable, informal positioning of furniture elements and, weather permitting, the fluid division between indoor and outdoor space.

Above Low armchair designed by Charles Eames with a moulded polyester seat on a wire substructure, 1950. Eames's new approach to seat furniture design was characterized by the quite separate consideration of seat unit and supportive structure.

Right Drawing submitted by Charles Eames and Eero Saarinen for their 'Relaxation Chair' in the Museum of Modern Art 'Organic Design in Home Furnishings' competition, 1940.

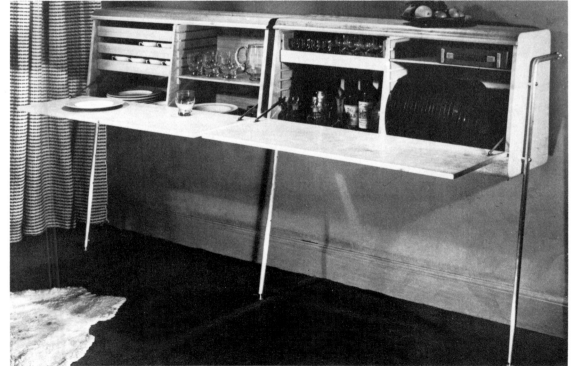

Above 'New Furniture Designed by Charles Eames', a view of the installation by Eames for the Museum of Modern Art's 1946 exhibit of his latest designs.

Left A prize-winning storage unit designed by Robin Day and Clive Latimer for the Museum of Modern Art's 'Low Cost Furniture' competition of 1948. The design of these units reflects the preoccupation with the counter-balance of mass and slender support which characterizes so much furniture of the immediate post-war years.

United States

The most prominent figure in the story of modern American furniture is Charles Eames. Born in 1907, Eames studied architecture at the Washington University, St Louis, and from 1930 ran his own design office in St Louis. His acceptance in 1936 of a fellowship at the Cranbrook Academy under Eliel Saarinen marked a significant new phase in his career. Here he became acquainted with the talented designers who were, with Eames, to become leading figures in post-war design. In 1937 he became head of the Department of Experimental Design.

Among his Cranbrook colleagues was Eero Saarinen, son of Eliel, with whom he collaborated in the preparation of the revolutionary series of designs which were to make the Museum of Modern Art's 'Organic Design in Home Furnishings' such a key event in the evolution of modern furniture. In 1940 Eames married and the following year he and his wife, Ray, moved to Venice, California, where he pursued the experiments in forms and materials which he had launched so successfully in 1940.

The 1940 projects brought several fresh ideas to furniture design, notably in the area of seat furniture for which Eames adopted the approach of considering independently, in view of their quite distinct functions, the two parts of a chair, the seating shell and the supportive sub-structure. For the shell Eames and Saarinen used plywood in a revolutionary way, not satisfied merely to curve it in one direction as Aalto had done, but moulding it in complex multi-directional curves which allowed a remarkable degree of flexibility. Legs were reduced to a minimum. For the 1940 competition, slender wooden legs were used, soon to be superseded by the steel-rod legs which were to become a hallmark of the Eames style.

Several of Eames's seat shells carry through the idea of multi-directional curves to a point where they become fascinating sculptural exercises in the free forms which were to be a dominant stylistic feature of post-war design. The 'Relaxation' chair and, more especially, the asymmetrical, amoeboid 'Lounging' chair of 1940 exemplify this concern with 'organic' form. In 1948 Eames designed a prototype Chaise which survives as perhaps his most purely sculptural exercise.

Nineteen-forty was important also for the Eames–Saarinen competition submission of modular storage units, an idea which was to be much copied. Standard-size cabinet units with assorted combinations of shelf, drawer or cupboard could be placed in a variety of arrangements on standardized low table bases.

Below left Dining chair with tilting back designed by Charles Eames, 1946.

Below Armchair designed by Charles Eames in moulded polyester and steel rod, 1950; the figure is the work of American cartoonist Saul Steinberg.

Design for modular storage units submitted by Charles Eames and Eero Saarinen in the 1940 Museum of Modern Art 'Organic Design in Home Furnishings' competition. These units were to set the pattern for a type of furniture which was to become increasingly fashionable through the forties and fifties. The modular concept represents a major development in the evolution of modern furniture.

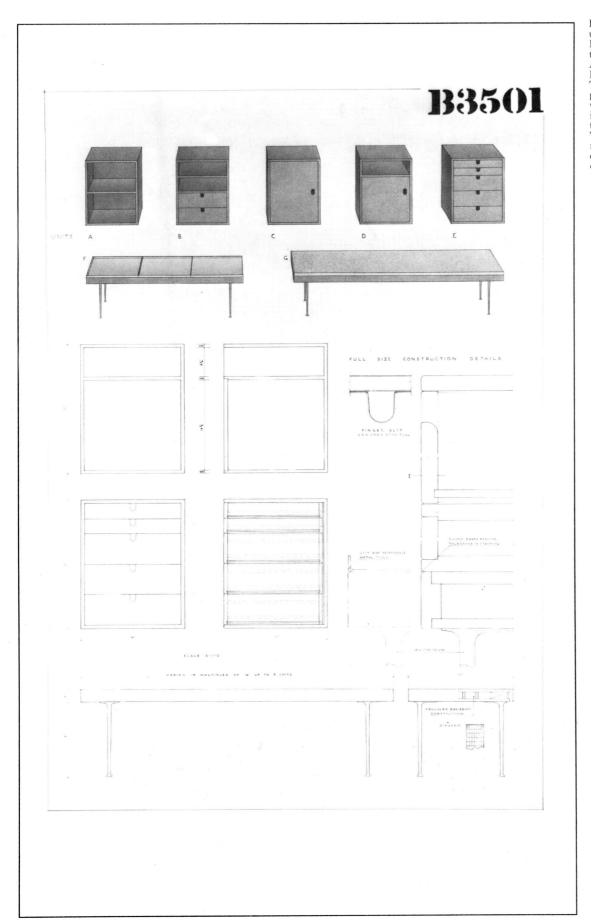

United States

Below Lounge Chair and Ottoman designed in 1956 by Charles Eames and perhaps the best known of all his chair designs. The leather-upholstered seat, arm and back units in a three-part cradle of rosewood ply with cast aluminium base and support elements combine in a luxurious and complex expression of Eames's distinctive style.

Opposite above Explanatory drawing showing the construction of Eames's Lounge Chair and Ottoman of 1956.

Opposite below right Folding screen design by Charles Eames in 1946; the moulded ash plywood panels are joined by canvas strips.

Eames will always be associated, however, above all with his now-classic 'Lounge Chair 670' of 1956. More complex in its design than is usual for Eames, this chair nonetheless expresses so many of his ideals. Its construction is frank, the structure exposed, yet in its emphasis on curves it suggests an informality that allows flexibility of placement. Typically, the cast aluminium base is considered quite separately from the rosewood-and-leather seat unit.

Perhaps less well known, but a particularly pleasing design, is Eames's plywood screen of 1946. Made of six panels of curving plywood linked by canvas strip hinges, the open screen forms a serpentine wall of considerable elegance.

Eames was foremost in a generation of American designers and a few enlightened manufacturers which somehow managed to find a new stylistic guise for the ideals of pre-war Modernism. They avoided the more extreme indulgences of style of the euphoric post-war period, applying themselves in a logical and committed way to the task of creating a softer second phase of Modernism.

Eero Saarinen, who had shared the glory with Eames for their prize-winning designs of 1940, went on to explore his own version of Organic Modernism, designing furniture for Knoll Associates from 1946. In 1950 he set up his own design office, Eero Saarinen Associates, in Michigan. This Finn, whose education had included a year studying sculpture in Paris, was to launch through the re-styled Knoll International a series of designs for tables and chairs which are amongst the most gracious exercises in the curvilinear Modernist style.

This range of 'Tulip' chairs and their complementary tables was first manufactured in 1957. The chairs had shells of glass fibre and column stems and flared circular bases of aluminium, all white and drawn in an unbroken series of fluid curves. The tables were designed in varying sizes and heights to suit every purpose with the option of tops in natural wood or elegant white marble. Saarinen wrote of this 'Pedestal' range, 'As to the pedestal furniture, the undercarriage of chairs and tables in a typical interior makes an ugly, confusing, unrestful world. I wanted to clear up the slum of legs.' Saarinen used new technologies and an artistic sensibility to create a new, plastic version of International Modernism.

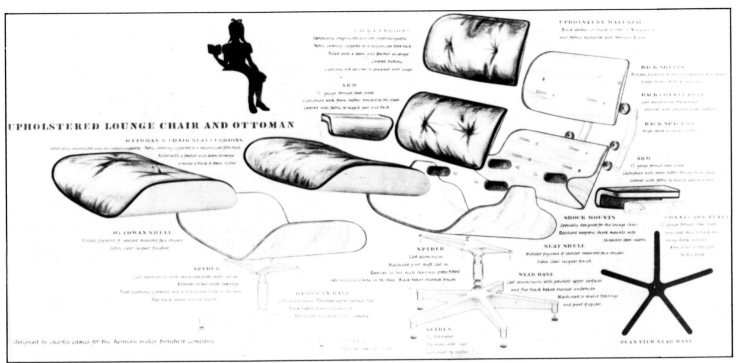

Left 'Tulip' chair designed by Eero Saarinen, manufactured by Knoll, 1957. The reinforced plastic seat and aluminium pedestal base combine in a fluid design of considerable beauty which has become as much a classic as Eames's Lounge Chair.

United States

The company founded by Hans and Florence Knoll was to prove one of the most progressive furniture manufacturers of the post-war era. Knoll spread itself internationally, opening branches in Germany and France in 1951 and establishing the British company Form International in 1970. Amongst Knoll's talented protégés was the sculptor Harry Bertoia who was engaged in 1950 with an open brief to pursue experiments in design. He developed a range of visually light chairs constructed of welded steel rods which were put into production in the early fifties and which have since been manufactured in considerable numbers.

Foremost in propagating the new furniture styles born of new technological developments was the American firm Herman Miller, which worked in close collaboration with Charles Eames after 1946 and which found in George Nelson both a talented design director and spokesman. In 1948 Nelson prepared a catalogue of the firm's designs and discussed the corporate philosophy, a philosophy which, he said, was '... so deeply felt that to the best of my knowledge, it has never been formulated.'

Amongst the most stylish expressions of Organic Modernism was the series of tables designed in the forties by sculptor Isamu Noguchi for Herman Miller. The plate-glass tops of these elegant tables are supported on free-form sculpted bases. The modular furniture explored in 1940 by Eames and Saarinen was to become a major feature of the Herman Miller production programme for both domestic and contract use. It was also to make a major contribution towards the development of the Contemporary style which crystallized through the fifties as the pre-dominant international 'good taste' style in furniture design and interior decoration for the middle class.

Harry Bertoia's 'Chickenwire' chairs and Eero Saarinen's marble-topped pedestal table combine in an interior scheme. The picture windows and flat overhanging roof have their source in the 'California Style' of Richard Neutra and his contemporaries.

Left Low table designed by the sculptor Isamu Noguchi for Herman Miller. The bowed triangular plate-glass top is raised on a base of two elements sculpted in walnut.

Below left 'Contour' lounge chair designed by Vladimir Kagan *c.* 1955 and manufactured by Kagan-Dreyfuss Inc.; walnut legs, deep foam rubber upholstery covered in black and white chenille texture fabric designed by Hugo Dreyfuss. Both this chair and the free-form table by Paul Laszlo (below) demonstrate the strong influence of Knoll and Miller on Modernist American furniture design of the fifties.

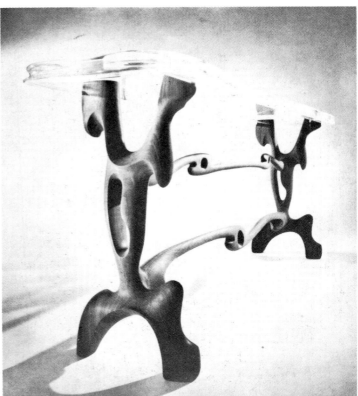

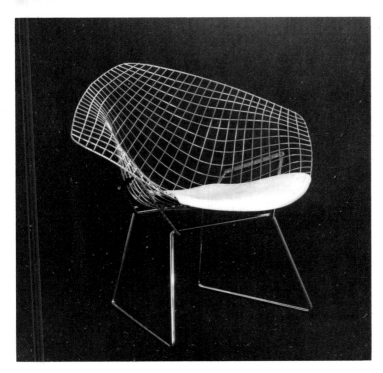

Left Chair design by Harry Bertoia. One of a series of designs evolved by the sculptor Bertoia after being given an open brief by Hans and Florence Knoll in 1950. 'If you will look at them, you will find that they are mostly made of air, just like sculpture. Space passes right through them,' wrote their designer.

Above Table designed by Paul Laszlo for Laszlo Inc. *c.* 1953. The free-form clear Lucite top is raised on legs sculptured in walnut by F. F. Kern, the forms of which seem to reflect the melting curves in Dali's desert landscapes.

United Kingdom

British designers, restricted by the Utility scheme, turned an envious eye to American design in the forties and when, in 1949, limitations were removed, many of the most progressive British designs showed a strong debt to pioneering American work. The *Studio Year Book* of 1949 illustrated '... one or two interesting results of modern experiments, notably in techniques born of the discovery that dissimilar materials can now be firmly bonded together.' One very specific example of the debt to American design was Dennis Young's 'Shell' chair of 1947–8. Its 'Fibrenyl' jute-reinforced thermoplastic frame on steel-rod base is descended directly from Eames's and Saarinen's 1940 designs, though the designer, writing in 1970, claimed that the chair was developed from anthropometric data provided by specific experimental research.

Thinness of structural elements was a popular borrowing from America, although it was used in some rather curious contexts within essentially traditional silhouettes. The prime example is Ernest Race's 'Antelope' chair designed in 1950 and used extensively on the South Bank the following year in the Festival of Britain. The chair is in effect a traditional Windsor executed in a material then in vogue and falsely suggesting a novelty of design. A curious compromise, the 'Antelope' was nonetheless a popular design and won a silver medal when exhibited at the Milan Triennale of 1954.

The post-war British taste for traditional forms was to be seen in the immense popularity of the variants on the classic Windsor designed by Lucien Ercolani under the Ercol trademark. Featured in the 'Britain Can Make It' exhibition of 1946, Ercol's suites have been in uninterrupted production ever since and their popularity is undiminished, though today they are associated with a strongly conservative taste. The traditional British love of deep-upholstered seat furniture was well catered for with such designs as those by Howard Keith for H.K. Furniture or by Ernest Race for Race Furniture. Keith made a feature of padded 'wings' on armchairs, whilst Race used deep buttoning as a deliberately traditional feature. Race was equally open to innovation and to the intelligent exploitation of new techniques and ideas. In 1945 he designed his B.A. chair specifically to use resmelted aluminium alloy from wartime scrap. He won a gold medal at the Milan 1951 Triennale for this design of which over a quarter of a million examples were made: an elegant solution to a practical problem.

Right 'Shell' chair designed by Dennis Young, 1947-8. The separate treatment of the 'Fibrenyl' thermoplastic shell and the steel-rod base reflect the influence of Eames.

Below Wing armchair designed by Ernest Race, late 1940s. This type of buttoned, upholstered wing chair enjoyed considerable popularity in post-war Britain, a popularity based on the reassuring character of an essentially traditional design.

Below right Rocking chair designed by Ernest Race in 1949 with steel-rod frame.

Left Chairs manufactured by Figli di Amadeo Cassino and designed by Gianfranco Frattini (top), Ico Parisi (centre), Carlo de Carli (bottom left) and Gio Ponti (bottom right); stylish examples of the new furniture styles which emerged from post-war Italy.

Below Music room in the Hotel Méditerranée at San Remo with furniture designed by Renzo Zavanella, late 1940s.

Above Fully upholstered reclining easy chair designed by Carlo Mollino c. 1949 and manufactured by Cellerino of Turin. A curious blend of the surreal and the streamlined in a stylish design from the most sculpturally inventive of the post-war Italian furniture designers.

Right Glass-topped table with wooden side members linked by metal strain rods and raised on sculptured legs, designed by Carlo Mollino and manufactured by Apelli & Varesio, before 1949.

France

This exuberant phase in Italian design, which paved the way for the present Italian supremacy, makes a strong contrast with the post-war years in French furniture. French designers, so influential in the twenties, were for the most part living on their past glories, with the Union des Artistes Modernes struggling bravely, but without inspiration, to bring to the French public an awareness of new technical and stylistic developments, inspired directly by American work. The regular 'Formes Utiles' exhibits of the U.A.M. through the fifties demonstrate the barrenness of this group of designers, several of whom had been such stylish exponents of Modernism before the war. The materials are poor, the designs derivative and France's furniture industry was not well adapted to series production. When, in 1955, the U.A.M. celebrated its quarter century with the publication of a survey of its achievements, the contemporary innovations included much use of *rattan*, or basket work, and the fashionable contrasts of thin structure and mass. The prominent designers, among them René Herbst (president of the group), Louis Sognot, Charlotte Perriand, Jean Prouvé and Marcel Gascoin were exploring post-war trends without managing to imbue their work with the sense of conviction which had given such a sparkle to their pre-war designs.

The French furniture industry was still for the most part oriented towards the cult of the individual *ébéniste*, the concept of series-production furniture going against the instincts of the French bourgeois mentality. The post-war years were uneasy transitional ones for a craft which was to all practical purposes extinct, and within which, despite attempts at innovation, there was no fundamental development. Novelties included most notably the extensive use of hide, often almost completely covering furniture and making a feature of saddle-stitched seams. The name of Jacques Adnet is strongly associated with this fashion. Dupré Laffon was one of the more prominent amongst the post-war furniture designers in the traditional spirit, whilst Jean Royère earned a reputation for the restrained dignity of his furniture and decorative schemes.

Interior of a hunting lodge designed by Jacques Adnet for the exhibition 'Le Génie de Paris'. The seat furniture, with hide-covered cushions on tubular metal frames, designed by Adnet, the table by Noll, the tapestry by Dominguez; published in 1952 in *Décor et Aménagement de la Maison*.

In the United States the market for luxurious cabinet furniture was well catered for by Tommi Parzinger whose 'Parzinger Originals' designs are more akin to French conservatism than the prevalent American spirit of innovation.

The forties and early fifties were complex years in the evolution of furniture design. Despite a strong lead from America, a readiness to experiment in Britain, a surprise flowering of Italian talent, there was no one universal style, though soft, curved forms had for the most part come to dominate design. Many designers carried Organic Modernism to stylistic extremes, others were reluctant to abandon tradition altogether in search of a truly contemporary style. While Americans had prepared the way for a new Modernism, it was Scandinavian designers who, during the fifties, were perhaps the most internationally influential in shaping a popular look in furniture and interior design. These two key threads came together to make the dominant looks of the fifties and early sixties, the Contemporary style and a revival of International Modernism.

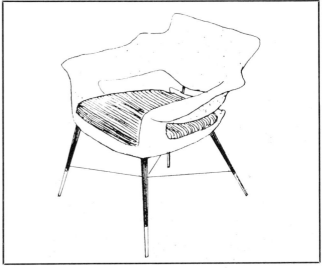

Above left Parisian living room decorated by Jean Royère c. 1952. The fireplace is of red brick, the corner settee and chairs are covered in green fabric. The base of the floor lamp is painted in orange.

Left 'Meuble Universel' and other furnishings designed by Jacques Dumond in collaboration with André Monpoix, 1952. The 'Meuble Universel' is a double-sided storage/display unit which also serves as a room divider.

Top Commode designed by Tommi Parzinger c. 1950 for the Charak Furniture Co., entirely covered in top grain leather and resting on a base of Korina wood. The doors have gold-tooled lattice decoration and brass ring handles – an exercise in elaboration more in keeping with post-war French furniture design.

Above Design for a chair by Jacques Gadoin in plywood and metal rod with wire stretchers. The influence of Eames is discernible in the cut-out back allowing multi-directional flexibility. Published in 1952.

The Fifties
The Contemporary Style

The fifties saw the coming of a distinctive 'Contemporary' look in furniture design – the establishment of a rationalized style on an international scale. It was a mature phase which emerged from the confusing diversity of the post-war years, rejecting stylistic extremes and elegantly distilling the ingredients of more sober influences, notably American and Scandinavian.

The Contemporary look became the expression of a new design awareness in a middle class which was at last enjoying the benefits of post-war prosperity. Never before, it would seem, had such a wide spectrum of the middle class been so self-conscious in matters of domestic good taste. Manufacturing and retail businesses had by now fully recovered from the crippling effects of the war and the West was entering an optimistic era of consumerism.

The Contemporary style in furniture design went hand in hand with new styles of living and domestic planning. The key concepts of the new style were fluidity and flexibility of interior space and the trend towards the incorporation of storage space into structural design eliminated the need for most traditional items of cabinet furniture. Typical of fifties interiors were modular, lightly-constructed wall storage/display units or versatile free-standing units which allowed a flexible use of space within a room.

The links between architecture and furniture design were significant ones. New fashions in domestic architecture were a response to less formal life styles which, in turn, demanded fluid and easy furniture. Similarly, the resurgence of International Modernism in the field of corporate architecture throughout the affluent period of the fifties and sixties encouraged the revival of International Modernist furniture styles, giving to sleek steel and leather furniture prestigious connotations which were in many ways directly opposed to the egalitarian, functionalist philosophies at the source of the style.

The fifties witnessed an unprecedented expansion of middle-class consumerism and televisions became a popular status symbol. Their casings were often designed by prominent furniture or industrial designers.

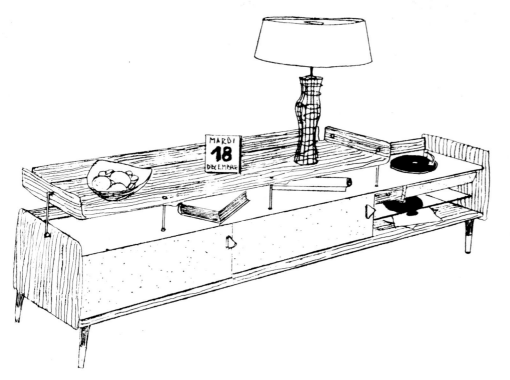

Left French commode with the long, low lines characteristic of fifties domestic furnishings.

Below Robin Day's 'Form' seating for Hille. Designed in 1957 this captures both the self-consciousness and the sophistication of the Contemporary Style. The lines are almost Japanese in their austere purity.

United States

America led the way in post-war architecture most
significantly in the corporate sector, but also in the
domestic field. In Richard Neutra West Coast
patrons found a gifted architect who was a prime
figure in the evolution of the 'California style' of
domestic architecture. The ingredients were flat,
overhanging roofs and vast plate-glass picture
windows which broke down the distinctions between indoor and outdoor areas. The fluid spaces
thus created demanded minimal and informal
furniture and Charles Eames' designs, 'organic' in
every sense, fitted easily into these schemes.

The pre-war move to America of Mies van der
Rohe and Gropius had made of the United States
the new centre of the International Modernist
ideology and it was not long before American
skylines were to be dominated by a new generation
of skyscrapers, sleek and simple monoliths in glass,
steel and concrete.

Leaders in the field of contemporary furniture,
and instrumental in changing the appearance of
furniture both for domestic and office or public use,
were the firms of Herman Miller and Knoll
International.

The emergence in the forties of Herman Miller,
under the design directorship of George Nelson, as
a pioneering firm in furniture design was one of the
key factors in the development of post-war furniture. Charles Eames designed for Herman Miller
from 1946 and the originality of his ideas and the
major stylistic innovations with which he is quite
justly credited have perhaps overshadowed the
achievements of Nelson himself as a designer and
of the others who contributed to the firm's success.

Eames, however, was the most influential figure
in the Herman Miller team. His modular storage
units of 1940, designed with Saarinen, were the
source of countless variants, designed by Eames
and others, which became a major production line
and the basis of thinking for the modular concept of
office furnishing. In the fifties Eames designed a
new range of seat furniture which marked an
evolution from his earlier, more organic, phase and
which might be regarded as the direct descendant
of pre-war Modernist designs. He moved away from
the slender rod structures, favoured in the forties,
to more substantial structures of cast aluminium
or chromium-plated steel; the curves of seats
became less emphatically anthropomorphic. An
early exercise in the new direction was his sofa of
1954 which has been described as '. . . svelte and
Spartan . . . one of the few original solutions to a

Eames 2

Chairs by Charles Eames:
clockwise from **top left:**
Lounge Chair, 1958; Armchair,
1971; Sofa, 1954; Dining Chair,
1946; Lounge Chair and
Ottoman, 1956.

particularly difficult problem of furniture design,' while the major venture in this new genre was the so-called 'Aluminium' group of chairs of 1958.

George Nelson was responsible for a number of stylishly eccentric creations which belie the fundamental sincerity of his approach to design. Among these must be counted his 'Marshmallow' sofa and 'Coconut' chair of 1956. The sofa has a seat and back made up of a total of eighteen padded cylinders on a slender metal base, while the chair is a sharply-cut segment on a steel-rod base.

Perhaps less memorable but certainly more influential was Nelson's B.S.C. or Basic Storage Components range which introduced a new versatility to the market. Herman Miller invested in research to evolve practical work furniture and these researches led to the establishment in 1960 of a Research Corporation under the direction of Robert Propst. This group explored the ergonomics of furniture design and, with an amalgam of Propst's ideas and Nelson's design concepts, led to the launch of a series of Action Office schemes which brought together both the functionalist ideals and stylistic characteristics of Inter-

national Modernism in the context of office design.

Knoll International spread its wings in the fifties and the firm's growth paralleled the resurgence of Modernism. Besides promoting the contemporary work of its own designers, who included notably Saarinen and Bertoia, Knoll started in the mid fifties to manufacture under licence the classic pre-war designs of Mies van der Rohe. His 'Barcelona' chair of 1929 had by then acquired a symbolic status as perhaps the supreme expression of the Bauhaus style, simple to the point of austerity, perfect in its proportions and discreetly luxurious.

Reissued by Knoll, the 'Barcelona' became a status symbol, a statement of design consciousness, and was to be found both in domestic interiors and in such prestige settings as embassies or company office foyers and reception rooms. Knoll's takeover of the Italian firm of Gavina meant that the company took over at the same time the manufacture of Marcel Breuer's pre-war designs. Knoll International has provided a complete decorating service and created a luxurious, understated look since the fifties, combining pre-war classics with the best of contemporary Modernism.

Scandinavia

The major difference between pre-war Modernism
and the revived Modernism of the fifties was the
addition in the latter of a feeling of discreet luxury
and a mellowness which was seldom present in the
pioneering pre-war era. While American firms and
designers perhaps did most to promote the new
sleek look, the mellowness, the softening of the
cold lines was above all the result of Scandinavian
influences.

Before the war Scandinavian designers had
preached a more humanistic mode of functionalism, rejecting what was seen as the clinical and
essentially hostile appearance of Bauhaus furniture and working towards a style which was based
on a respect for tradition and, in particular, on a

respect for the traditional material of the furniture
craft – wood. The Dane, Kaare Klint, and the Finn,
Alvar Aalto, were perhaps the most influential
precursors of what was to become a major international influence in the fifties.

The furniture industries of Denmark, Finland
and Sweden, in particular, were greatly encouraged after the war by official concern to
maintain good standards of design and production.
In Sweden the Slöjdföreningen was an official body
with the task of implementing a democratic functionalism by encouraging consumer awareness
and good relations between designers and manufacturers. The publication of a consumer's guide,
the *Möbelräd*, a book of suggestions and standards

in furniture design, proved beneficial to public and industry alike.

Carl Malmsten has been described as the father of modern Swedish furniture. Certainly, his liberal socialist idealism and his aim, inspired in part by national tradition and the theories of the Arts and Crafts Movement, of combining harmoniously the demands of function and visual pleasure, were at the very basis of the Scandinavian Modern style. Malmsten's furniture, like that of another influential Swede, Bruno Mathsson, whose career also started before the Second World War, is interesting and praiseworthy for its timelessness. Both designers evolved a subtle, mellow style which avoided extremes of fashion.

Malmsten's dictum that 'Moderation lasts, Extremism palls' was proved right by his own work and by that of Mathsson. Notable amongst Malmsten's pupils is the designer Karl Erik Ekselius whose furniture is a refined rationalization of modern needs and traditional craft. Mathsson is perhaps best known for a long experimentation, started in the thirties, in the evolution of an ergonomically sound range of laminated wood-framed seat furniture. He has favoured unstained beech, a native wood, and made a feature of woven leather strips for upholstery. His classic designs are still, with only minor changes, in production today and are manufactured as before by the firm founded at Varnamo by his father, Karl Mathsson.

Chair designed by Bruno Mathsson for Karl Mathsson Varnamo. This is one of several variants on a highly successful design, the original of which was first produced in 1934 and which has come to be regarded as the definitive expression of Mathsson's style.

Denmark

The war years which were so crippling to the Scandinavian furniture industries were, ironically, not without advantage in the history of Danish furniture. The occupation years saw an introspective and reassuring involvement in the craft traditions of work in wood. The teachings of Klint and the revitalization of the Danish Cabinetmakers' Guild as an exhibition society in 1927 had spearheaded the revival of interest in craft furniture. After the war, with high standards maintained by official bodies, Danish furniture was soon to earn an international respect and win an eager international market. In their display galleries, Den Permanente, in Copenhagen, Denmark's designers have a showcase for their work which in turn encourages high standards in design and manufacture.

Aware of the importance of consistently high standards the Danish furniture industry wisely set up its own watchdog, the Danish Furniture Manufacturers' Quality Control Board, which submits all new designs to rigorous tests. Denmark's Society of Arts and Crafts and Industrial Design involves itself in the promotion of good design, sponsoring experimental work.

If Klint represents the philosophical ideals behind the renaissance of Danish furniture after the war, no single designer better expressed in his work the true spirit of that renaissance than Hans Wegner. Trained at the Copenhagen School of Arts and Crafts and later opening his own office in 1943 at Gentofte, Wegner soon emerged as a leading artist, whose work was remarkable for its combination of effortlessly graceful forms and painstaking concern for the crafting of these forms in wood.

The characteristic feature of his chair designs is in the sweeping movement of back rail and arms carved as one single form. His definitive design of 1949, known at once simply and emphatically as 'The Chair', has been described as '. . . the ultimate in painstaking thought and workmanship.'

The capable cabinet-making firm of Johannes Hansen was entrusted with the series production of his meticulously crafted prototypes. Wegner's mellow style, modern in its functionalism and uncluttered lines, while at the same time strongly rooted in tradition, struck the right balance. This was the style which found for Denmark a major export market for furniture.

Below right The 'AX chair 6003', designed by Peter Hvidt and Oria Molgaard-Nielsen in 1950 and manufactured by Fritz Hansen, laminated beech frame, teak seat and back. This chair won a Diploma of Honour when included in the Milan Triennale Exhibitions of 1951 and 1954.

Above 'Windsor' style chair designed by Hans Wegner.

Right Plywood and steel-rod
stacking chair designed by
Arne Jacobsen and
manufactured by Fritz Hansen.

Mogensen/Juhl

Børge Mogensen and Finn Juhl were contemporaries of Wegner's who each evolved personal variants on the Contemporary Danish style. Mogensen was very much concerned with standards of size and construction for modular storage furniture and designed cabinet elements for the firm of Boligens Byggeskabe which were first exhibited in 1954. Although as adept in the use of wood as his contemporaries, Mogensen was principally motivated in his search for forms by the rationalized requirements of mass-production. Juhl's work, on the other hand, shows a strong fascination with sculptural forms, though he never abandoned the guiding principles of functionalism. Juhl evolved confident, free forms for seat furniture, in which the sweeping sensuous curves of seats, backs and armrests have the added function of making them inviting.

Another exponent of the sculptural free form, and an influential figure in the story of Danish furniture, is Arne Jacobsen, a versatile designer whose career began in the twenties and who came to international prominence as one of the most stylish exponents of the Danish Contemporary school. In the early fifties he launched his first single-unit ply seat on steel-rod chairs, very much in the style of Eames but with a distinctive personal touch in the silhouette of the ply seat. These full curves were carried to their logical conclusion in two designs dating from the late fifties which soon acquired a strong iconographic significance – the 'Swan' and 'Egg' chairs. Jacobsen's designs were manufactured by the firm of Fritz Hansen.

In Poul Kjaerholm, Denmark had a designer who, in the fifties and sixties, gave a new slant to the use of metal for furniture, evolving a mellow and highly sophisticated version of International Modernism, and softening the coldness of the metal with the use of natural materials such as wood, cane and hide. As designer to the manufacturing firm of E. Kold Christiensen of Copenhagen, Kjaerholm has produced a stylish range with elegant, minimal frameworks or limbs of steel; most distinctively he used flat rather than tubular steel, as did Mies van der Rohe, and his designs have been promoted by Knoll International, foremost advocates of the International Modernist ideals of furniture design.

Below Desk and Chair designed by Finn Juhl.

Right 'Egg' chair designed by Arne Jacobsen, leather upholstered and swivelling on a cast aluminium base, manufactured by Fritz Hansen, 1958.

Opposite 'Swan' Chair designed by Arne Jacobsen, leather upholstered and swivelling on a cast aluminium base, manufactured by Fritz Hansen, 1958.

Finland

Scandinavian design was propagated in the fifties and sixties through international exhibitions, such as the exhibition 'Design in Scandinavia', which opened in the United States in 1954, 'Formes Scandinaves', at the Musée des Arts Décoratifs, Paris in 1958, 'Neue Form aus Danemark', in Germany in 1956–7, 'The Arts of Denmark' in the United States in 1960–1, 'Finlandia', shown in Zurich, Amsterdam and London in 1961 and, of course, the regular Milan Triennales at which the strength of Finnish design in particular was first internationally appreciated.

After the sterility of the war years, Finland's designers returned to the international scene with a remarkable display of strength, a sense of unity in the creation of sophisticated new forms of a restrained elegance. The leading furniture manufacturers were the firms of Artek and Asko Finnternational. Alvar Aalto founded Artek in 1935 to manufacture his ply and laminated wood designs, then pursued his experiments after the war, increasing the range of designs and refining details within the skills perfected before the war.

Finland's furniture industry was geared to mass-production, and did not have the emphasis on craft which so distinguished Danish work. Amongst Aalto's post-war designs, perhaps the most satisfying is the stool of 1954 in which the laminate legs fan out elegantly into the seat. In Finland as in Denmark, official promotion and quality controls have assured the export success of the furniture industry. This support has come through the relevant ministries, through Ornamo (the Association of Industrial Designers), the Finnish Foreign Trade Association and the Finnish Society of Crafts and Design.

When, in the fifties, International Modernism came once again to the fore as a major ingredient of the Contemporary look, Finland found two particularly able exponents of the style in Ilmari Tapiovaara and Antti Nurmesniemi. Tapiovaara had, indeed, spent a part of his training in the office of Le Corbusier and, though he did not completely reject the use of traditional local woods as used by Aalto, both he and Nurmesniemi were more in their element in designing metal furniture for commercial mass-production or for prestigious high quality series production.

'Corner of a Finnish Living Room', wool-covered settee, plane wood table with hinged magazine rack, the steel-rod and fabric chair designed by Marianne Boman for O/Y Boman A.B., illustrated in *The Studio Year Book of Decorative Art 1954-5*.

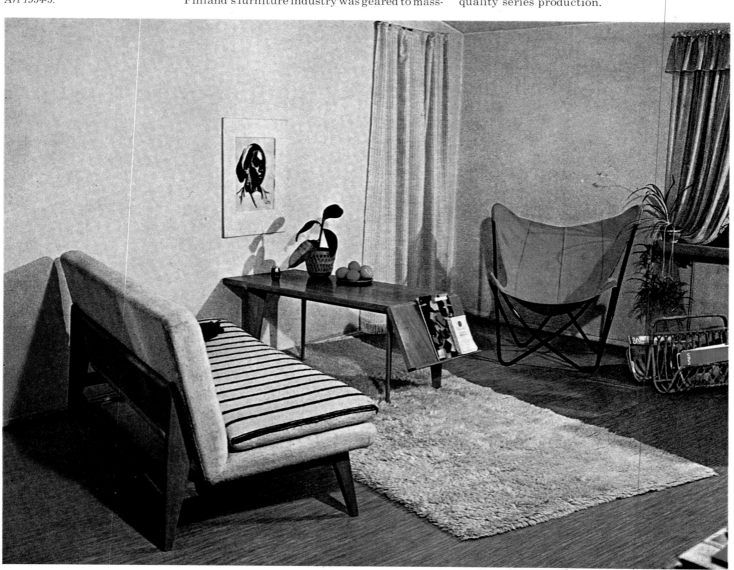

Tapiovaara

Above Stacking chair designed by Ilmari Tapiovaara, manufactured by Lukkiseppo Oy, Rekola. This chair, known as the 'Lukki I' and constructed of enamelled tubular steel and ply was first used in the Helsinki showroom of Olivetti.

Left Chair designed by Anti Nurmesniemi in 1960 and manufactured by J. Merivaara of Helsinki. When presented at the Milan Triennale of 1960 this design in chromium-plated steel and leather won its designer a gold medal.

United Kingdom 1

Above Easy chair with deep upholstered seat and back and table arms, designed by Robin Day and manufactured by Hille.

Below Seating designed for British Rail by Robin Day and manufactured by Hille. The design was specially considered to present a minimum risk of damage by vandals.

Scandinavian design became a major shaping force in the international development of a Contemporary look in the fifties. It was a force strongly felt in the United States but was perhaps even more influential in the United Kingdom: Eames and his contemporaries had already established their own forceful guidelines in American design in the forties.

In Britain, after the confusion of the first few years of freedom from Utility restrictions, a new Contemporary style took shape. The influence of both the United States and Scandinavia, though very much in evidence at the beginning of the period, was later superseded by the emergence of a distinctive, independent British style.

After the flush of enthusiasm of the Festival of Britain, there was still considerable room for improvement in the design-consciousness of British furniture manufacturers. A crucial event in the promotion of good design was the opening of the Design Centre in London's Haymarket in 1956 as a permanent showcase for British goods.

These were selected by the Design Index Committee according to a strict set of criteria relating to performance, safety, construction, ergonomics, aesthetics and cost. In the following year the Design Centre gave its first awards to goods selected by a panel which included R.Y. Gooden, Brian O'Rorke and R.D. Russell. Prominent among the winners was furniture designer Robin Day, designing for the progressive firm of Hille.

For Hille, Robin Day designed furniture that was the perfect epitome of the Contemporary look. Long, low lines predominated and the modular concept was very much in evidence, with countless variations made possible by the flexible use of standard component elements. His 'Form' seating and table range of 1957 is a classic example, pared down to essentials with an almost Japanese sense of discipline.

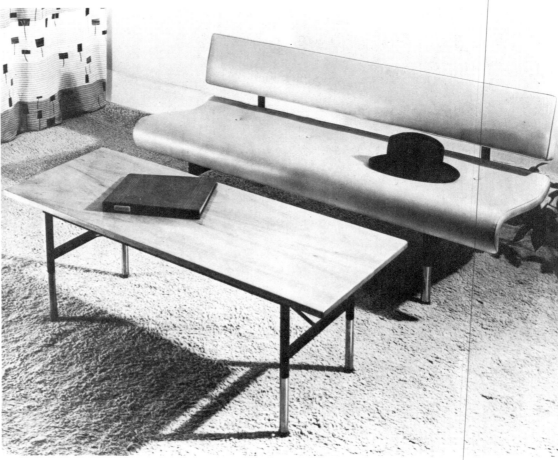

Cabinet/display unit designed by Robin Day in 1950 and shown at the Festival of Britain and at the Milan Triennale in 1951. The formica panel is the design of Geoffrey Clark and relieves Day's otherwise starkly simple style.

United Kingdom 2

The main ingredients of fifties Contemporary in Britain were long low lines in coffee tables, wood-framed sofas, wall fixtures and free-standing room-dividers or cabinets. the latter now designed to accommodate record player and record rack as well as drinks and glasses. The restrained lines, for the most part straight, were often softened by the curves of edges and corners. Despite the practicality of metal, wood was more popular and quality woods were used increasingly – not only the oiled teak copied from Danish furniture but such woods as afrormosia and rosewood. Prominent designers and manufacturers included Robert Heritage, designing for Archie Shine and Race Furniture; Ernest Race for his own company, Race Furniture; Dennis Young; Frank Guille; Professor R.D. Russell; John and Sylvia Reid for Stag; Terence Conran and the worthy but much caricatured G-Plan design team.

By the turn of the decade there was already a shift in taste towards a harder, more polished version of the Contemporary and metal enjoyed a renewed popularity in a style that reflected the increasing strength of the International Modernist revival. This trend was particularly marked in the contract sector, as a boom period in the economy reflected itself in the expensive furnishing of prestige business premises with the slick luxury of hide and metal.

Chromium-plated metal, aluminium and stainless steel were to become major ingredients of furniture design in the sixties. But above all the sixties was to be a decade of variety, a decade sparkling with new ideas, new forms, materials and colours in furniture design as designers and public alike tired of the restrictive notions of irreproachable good taste which had shaped the Contemporary look.

Interior of the sixties showing the lasting influence of the Contemporary style, one of the keys to which was a restrained and tasteful simplicity within fluid interior spaces.

Top left Suite of seat furniture designed by Ernest Race in 1957 in steel with leather and fabric upholstery. By the late fifties there was a more general use of richer quality materials than had been possible in the lean post-war years.

Top right 'Dormouse' sofa, designed by Ernest Race during the early fifties, with rod frame and rubber upholstery.

Above 'Hamilton' sideboard designed in 1958 by Robert Heritage for Archie Shine. Here are the characteristic long, low lines of the Contemporary Style.

The Sixties
Neo-Modernism to Pop

Below Apartment in Brussels, showing sixties taste for new forms and new materials; armchair by Joe Colombo, dining chairs by Thonet and table by Wabbes.

Below right Storage unit by the Conran Design team for Habitat. Practical, attractive designs at moderate prices were the ingredients of the Habitat success in exploiting a young, middle-class market.

So many forces combined to make the sixties a lively and fascinating decade in the arts, in technology and above all socially. Youth emerged as a strong market force; social taboos and traditions came under strong attack. An iconoclastic decade, the so-called 'Swinging Sixties' inevitably produced fashions and designs for furniture and domestic objects to match the mood, a mood which produced its most characteristic manifestations towards the middle of the decade.

The austerity of the forties had been left behind long ago and had by now faded from memory. The innovations of the fifties, from the bright-eyed optimism of the 'Festival (of Britain) Style' and its foreign equivalents to the smug good taste of the Contemporary Style seemed whimsical or timid.

Organic Modernism, apart from a few confident and lasting classics, seemed distinctly old-fashioned to a bright and energetic young generation with money to spend and a determination to make its own stylistic mark. For a variety of reasons, London was to become an international centre of this bubbling activity and artistic creativity. This was the brash decade of Pop Art and Pop culture and, even though clever marketing has made America's Pop artists more widely known, the movement had its strongest roots in the Independent Group at the Institute of Contemporary Arts in London.

The sixties was a decade of consolidated prosperity in the western economies, with little suggestion as yet of any threatening cloud on the horizon.

Although peppered with individual disasters and played to the background of the Vietnam war, progressively tarnishing an image of the United States which had been so bright and influential in terms of style in the previous decades, the sixties was a decade of technological adventure, as jet travel came into its own. It was a spirit of adventure symbolized by the Space Race, culminating just before the close of the decade in Man's first steps on the Moon.

These many facets of the era were reflected in attitudes to design and can be identified within the rich variety of furniture created in the decade. Pop Art suggested 'Pop' furniture, while Pop and Hard-Edge Abstractionism heralded new ideas on colour, often in new materials made available by the progress of technological research into synthetics. The mood of scientific adventure inspired 'Space Age' furniture styles. Youth, with its traditional concern with the present, encouraged the idea of disposability and 'fun' furniture and threw itself also with equal enthusiasm into nostalgic revival styles and, towards the close of the decade, into exotic escapist styles. Young, middle-class families found a safe, middle-of-the-road style of furnishing in the ubiquitous Habitat look, ably propagated by Terence Conran. The quiet heroes of the decade, pioneers of a new elegance combining quality and style in furniture manufacture, were the Italian designers who were to dominate the international market during the seventies and led the field in plastic furniture.

Below The blow-up seating in this futuristic house in the French countryside points to two dominant trends in the furniture design of the decade: fascination with Space Age forms and the new materials made available by a rapidly advancing technology.

Left The great classics of International Modernism still continued to find favour among designers and decorators of the sixties; Marcel Breuer's 'Wassily' chair in an eclectic setting in a Paris apartment.

Neo-Modernism

The strongest link of sixties furniture with the previous decade was in the persistence of the International Modernist revival. The decline of Organic Modernism was followed by the return of International Modernism in a chic new guise. Indeed, the sixties saw the consolidation of International Modernism in the vernacular of the decorative arts as a prestige style for furniture, dominating unequivocably the contract sector but once again widely apparent in domestic decoration. The open-plan spaces first exploited to such effect in domestic architecture after the war maintained their popularity through the sixties, though the hard edges of the new Modernist furniture demanded a stricter, more disciplined, less flexible use of space than was possible with the softer lines of Organic Modernism or Scandi-

navian-style Contemporary furniture.

An international survey of private houses published in 1967, despite the evident bias of the compiler, Werner Weidert, shows the pervasiveness of this look. A distinctive feature of this International Style, apart from the austere look of furniture in metal, glass, hide and plain fabric or wood, was the predominance of plain, undecorated wall surfaces, an austerity relieved occasionally by a contrasting wall of wood or bare brick.

As corporate offices soared skywards in a remarkable spate of high-rise building which had started in the fifties, the new Modernism became the style symbolic of success and modernity for the executive suite or foyer. The essential coldness of the style made it perhaps more appropriate to business or public furnishing than domestic decor-

Below The '928' range of seat furniture, designed in 1965 by Vico Magistretti and manufactured by Cassina. The simplicity of this elegant hide-covered suite carries on the best traditions of International Modernism.

Left 'Chair 20' designed in 1968 by Poul Kjaerholm and manufactured by E. Kold Christiensen A/S of Copenhagen. Kjaerholm was one of the most sophisticated of a new generation of International Modernist designers. This chair, in chromium-plated steel and ox-hide, is an elegant example of his work.

Opposite above left Modular Table T9/T10 and Tractor Stools T7/T8 designed and manufactured by O.M.K. Design Ltd, 1968. The firm of O.M.K. was prominent in the revival of tubular steel in the sixties, while the tractor seat stools anticipate the Industrial Style which was to become so prevalent in the late seventies.

Opposite 'Farmer Chair and Table', designed in 1966 by Gerd Lange and manufactured by Wilhelm Bofinger of Stuttgart. Constructed in ash with canvas seat and back, this chair, a second generation Modernist design, bears an uncanny resemblance to Bauhaus precursors in the emphatic angularity of its construction.

ation. The new Modernism found favour with numerous manufacturers and designers during the sixties.

The sixties saw the extensive revival of chromium-plated tubular metal for seat and table furniture. Stylish new designs came from the London studios of Zeev Aram and Associates and from the team of young designers who founded the O.M.K. studio in 1966. O.M.K. used a wider diameter tubing than that associated with Bauhaus precursors and achieved a distinctive look. Zeev Aram, in addition to marketing his own designs, has led the field in Britain with the manufacture under licence of Bauhaus and Le Corbusier classics. Aram has recently added a number of designs to this range from another pioneer of Modernism, Eileen Gray.

Left 'Pedestal' theatre seating system, designed by Peter Dickenson for Race Furniture. This design has the distinction of being the only furniture to be awarded the Duke of Edinburgh Award for Elegant Design in 1965. The contract sector has become increasingly a preoccupation of leading furniture designers.

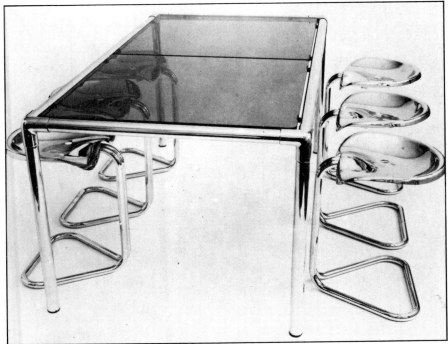

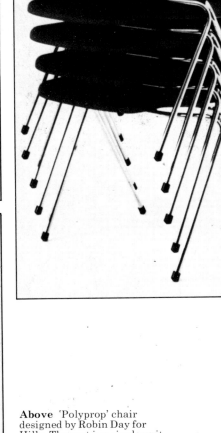

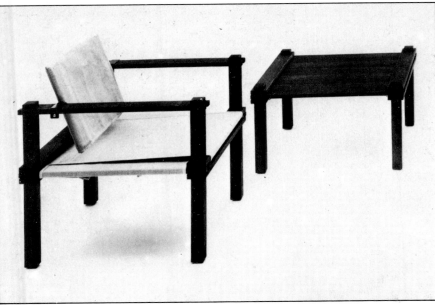

Above 'Polyprop' chair designed by Robin Day for Hille. The seat is a single unit of moulded polypropylene on steel-rod legs. Designed in 1963 and manufactured since then in vast numbers, this highly practical chair is the direct descendant of Eames's designs from the forties and fifties.

Sixties chairs

The revival of a new Modernism in the sixties was an international phenomenon. Among its most sophisticated exponents was Danish designer Poul Kjaerholm, a leading figure since the fifties in establishing the reputation of Scandinavian design. Kjaerholm's 'Hammock Chair 24' of 1965 is a particularly refined expression of his style and, like many of his designs, invites comparison with the work of his obvious mentor Mies van der Rohe.

Chair design acquired an increasingly symbolic role during the sixties, and the trends of the decade lend themselves to easy definition through the study of chair designs alone. The emphasis on chair design almost as a statement of faith amongst designers or architects has its roots in the classic designs which became so symbolic of Modernism in the twenties, its pre-history in Mackintosh's eccentric chairs and Rietveld's Red/Blue Chair, a truly sculptural manifesto.

The reduced need for cabinet furniture and the discipline of innovation within the necessary limitations of ergonomic factors increased the emphasis on chair design. This emphasis was further reinforced by a series of chair exhibitions

Group of chairs which, with the exception of one (extreme right), were all designed in 1967 or 1968. Left to right: 'Model 577' designed by Pierre Paulin, foam rubber and jersey on metal frame; 'Model 1159' designed by Jean-Pierre Laporte, painted plywood and polyester foam; red square pouffe and yellow quarter circle cushion designed by the Galeries Lafayette Studio, polyester foam and felt or jersey; chair (matching stool second from right) designed by Roger Tallon, polished aluminium and polyester foam; 'Chauffeuse IV 63' designed by Fabricious and Kastholm of Denmark, moulded wood, stainless steel and calfskin; steel prototype chair (foreground) designed by Jean-Philippe Charbonnier; 'Kaido' designed by Hugues Steiner, foam-covered frame and jersey; 'LA 1071' designed by Erwin Laverne, hide and metal (1955).

which included that held at the Stedelijk Museum, Amsterdam, in 1966, an exhibition at the Musée des Arts Décoratifs, Paris, in 1968 and the exhibition 'Modern Chairs 1918–1970' organized by the Victoria and Albert Museum in 1970 at the Whitechapel Art Gallery.

The strength of the Modernist image and the influence of Mies van der Rohe was well demonstrated in the work of the Italian studio, Archizoom Associati, formed in Florence in 1966. Archizoom paid a bizarre homage to the pioneer of Modernism in an extraordinary design of 1969,

the 'Mies' chair, an open wedge of steel, chromium-plated and with a stretched rubber sheet as seat. The Milan studio, Designers Associated, established in 1968, found novel forms for chromium-plated tubular steel. In the United States John Mascheroni used wide-gauge chromium-plated tubular steel in designs 'of a clean, positive architectural definition, which is enhanced by the sheer area of the reflective polished metal', according to the Whitechapel Gallery exhibition catalogue. The seventies, however, were to witness the decline of Modernism as a style in many circles.

Sixties Modernism/New Forms

After the dominance of the austerity of revived Modernism and the seriousness of the Contemporary look, elements both of fun and of fantasy were entering furniture design and interior decoration.

This reaction took on several guises which, once again, often found their most perfect expression in chair designs. The predominant desire was for an image of modernity, but it was a modernity of the Space Decade, anxious rather to explore the fantasy of the future than to continue to lean on the pioneer Modernists of the past. There was an increasing element of playfulness in the concept of furniture. A characteristic example of the new mood and a symbol of the period was Eero Aarnio's 'Globe' chair – a futuristic, spherical cocoon of fibre-glass; the inside was fully upholstered and was designed to swivel on a flared aluminium base. Designed for the leading Finnish manufacturers, Asko Finnternational, and launched in 1966, the eccentric but timely design of this chair assured its instant success.

Numerous designers explored variants on the futuristic seat module. Finnish designer Yrjö Kukkapuro, in independent practice since 1959, found a distinctive personal version of this style in his upholstered seats in moulded fibre-glass shells in futuristic forms.

'Globe' chair designed by Eero Aarnio for Asko Finnternational, 1966. The swivelling sphere is of fibre-glass, fully upholstered on the inside and raised on a flaring base of aluminium. This space-age chair was featured in a number of films and television films in the late sixties as a symbol of modishness.

Sixties Modernism/New Forms

The credit for designing furniture and interiors for the ultimate space fantasy film of the sixties, *2001: A Space Odyssey*, goes to French designer Olivier Mourgue who invented strange melting forms in polyether foam on a steel frame. In an article in *Vogue* in August 1966 on 'The Late Sixties Look' the author draws comparisons between fashionable colours in clothes and in furniture and interior decoration. Shiny white is singled out as the 'basic leveller of this age. It belongs strictly to the late sixties . . . No colour is more accommodating, no colour makes a better foil or background for hot orange, red, pink and violet whether moving around as a skimpy dress . . . or static as accent colours. Shiny white . . . with glossy vinyl-covered furniture, shiny floors and rather less shiny walls.' Aarnio's chair captured the look as others attempted to express it in words. This was the furniture style that corresponded to the futuristic fantasy of André Courrèges' startling fashions.

Magazines of the mid to late sixties were filled with images of space-age, push-button, remote controlled living in fantasy interiors. Even kitchens were now being designed like rocket control stations. In London, universal hub of the sixties dream, the firm of Zarach launched a novel variant on the coy television cabinets of the Contemporary era, enclosing the workings in clear perspex.

Left Materials and forms suggestive of the equipment and furnishings of space craft came to vogue in the late sixties – a trend encouraged by the increasing availability of durable plastics for furniture manufacture.

Left The Space Hilton from *2001: A Space Odyssey* (1968), furnished with jersey-covered chairs by Olivier Mourgue.

Sixties Modernism/New Materials

Below The Space Age look interpreted for Hille. It was a look which enjoyed considerable popularity in the decade of intensive space exploration and designs along similar themes appeared simultaneously in various countries.

Opposite Post-Modernist interior of the late sixties, incorporating perspex and acrylics, designed by Alexander Albrizzi for a London apartment.

This dream-like, futuristic side of the sixties seems distinctly *passé* a decade on and, on closer inspection, there are few designs of lasting merit within this fantasy phase. It was a mood perhaps better expressed in evocative staccato phrases than in serious creativity. Beneath the trendy novel shapes devised by such talented designers as Kukkapuro or Aarnio, and their equally progressive contempories, however, lies a more lasting aspect of their work, research into the potential of novel materials and notably of new synthetics.

The experimentations into synthetics applicable to the furniture industry, pioneered since the forties by Charles Eames and a few other designers, had already suggested possible new forms, as in Dennis Young's anthropomorphic 'Shell' chair of 1947-8. The eager return to the luxury of fine natural materials in the fifties, however, and the revived use of steel with the renascent Modernism, slowed the application of new synthetics as popular materials for domestic furniture design. The sixties, however, saw designers in search of novelty turning with renewed enthusiasm to synthetics, creating new shapes appropriate to the

materials, and, significantly, discovering a bright new palette, perfectly suited to the materials and in tune with the mood of current movements in the fine arts.

New materials exploited in the sixties included resilient but flexible plastics for the moulding of seat shells, tables and other basically rigid items, and synthetic upholstery materials which effectively rendered sprung upholstery obsolete.

London-based decorator Alexander Albrizzi produced elegantly simple furniture and furnishings in smoked, coloured or clear perspex and acrylics.

In a survey of late sixties interiors published in 1969, *Connaissance des Arts* illustrated a dining room decorated by Albrizzi for Mrs John Duffield in London. Here, certainly, are the crisp edges, the hard reflective surfaces of Modernism, but the intent is altogether different, more self-consciously decorative in concept and distinctively late sixties in feeling.

Swiss-based architect-designer Verner Panton designed a sixties classic in 1960, his celebrated single-unit moulded fibre-glass stacking chair, put into production in 1967.

Sixties Modernism/New Methods

A commercially significant feature of the exciting new forms was that they could be moulded on a production line at a fast rate. In Germany, for example, architect Helmut Bätzner designed a chair in 1966 as a single unit moulded in glass-fibre which could be made by the manufacturer Wilhelm Bofinger of Stuttgart at the rate of one every four minutes. The ever-inventive Eero Aarnio designed a worthy successor in 1968 to his 'Globe' chair of 1966. This was his 'Pastilli' chair, a progression from the glass-fibre and aluminium 'Globe' in being made entirely of glass-fibre, moulded in two halves, a swollen circular bubble with scooped seat and available in a variety of primary colours.

A number of French designers made interesting experiments with foam upholstery in this spate of renewed exploration into synthetics. Most prominent were designers Mourge, Roger Tallon and Pierre Paulin. Paulin and Mourge proved themselves great stylists, though Tallon came dangerously close to eccentricity with a range of designs using foam upholstery moulded in rows of uninviting soft mounds. In 1969 Laurent Dioptaz designed a chair which could double as a table. A simple cube of polyurethane foam covered in nylon jersey, its function as a seat only became evident as the sitter's weight depressed the bulk of the cube, leaving a standing angle as back and arms.

A more obviously functional successor to such designs was the 'Molecula' range of seat and table units designed by Robert Heritage and Roger Webb for Race International Designs Ltd. Seats and tables are moulded in the same resilient polyurethane foam and slot together in variable combinations to suit the locations. A publicity leaflet describes the range as having ' . . the character of soft sculptured forms combining texture and colour'. This range was finally marketed in 1978.

'Djinn Chaise Longue' designed by Olivier Mourgue in 1963 and manufactured by Airborne, Paris; tubular steel frame with polyether foam upholstery with removable nylon jersey covering.

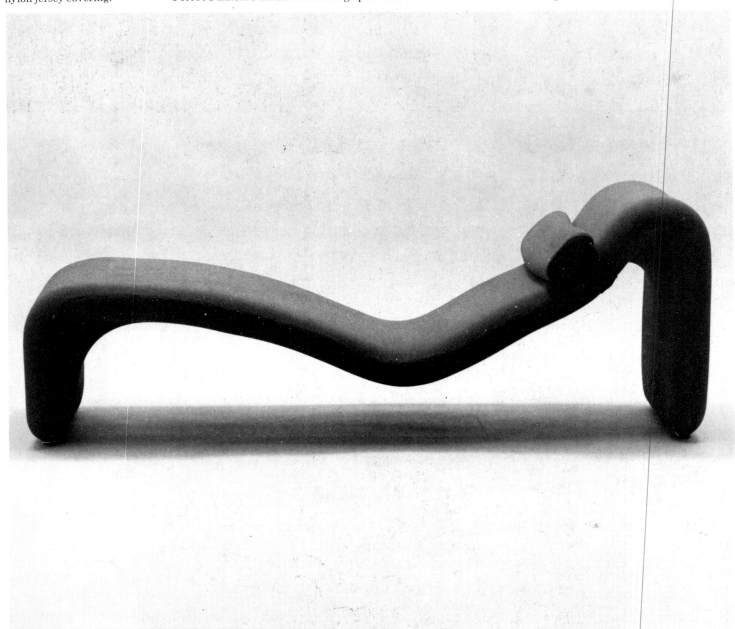

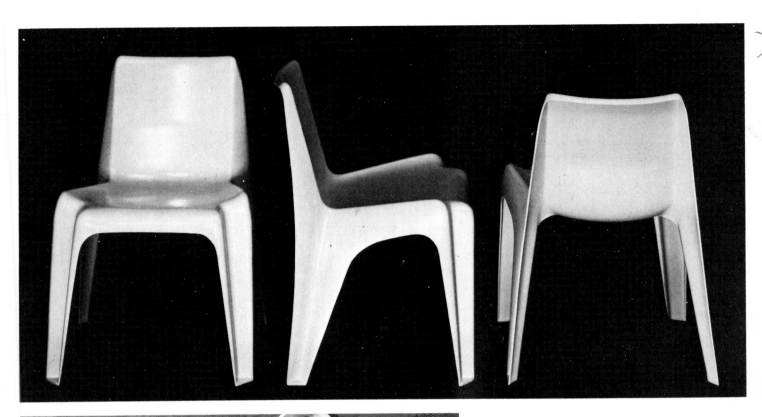

Above 'BA 1171 Chair' designed by Helmut Batzner in 1966 and manufactured by Wilhelm Bofinger of Stuttgart. This chair could be manufactured at the rate of one every four minutes. The design was widely exhibited and in 1966 won the Studio Rosenthal Prize.

Left Production-line manufacture of moulded seat units in man-made materials.

Popular Furniture of the Sixties/Habitat

Perhaps the most pervasive image of the sixties, extending itself internationally through the seventies and a remarkable marketing phenomenon, has been the Habitat look, brainchild of designer/entrepreneur Terence Conran. The first Habitat shop was opened in 1964, the start of a remarkable success story. Conran's aim was to bring good design to a wide market and to provide a choice of possible solutions to every domestic decoration problem, selling not just furniture but co-ordinating fabrics and papers, light fittings, kitchen equipment and domestic objects of every kind.

Habitat's mail-order catalogues demonstrate clearly the endeavour to bring both good and fashionable design, not always the same thing, to a wide public. The same catalogue advertises re-issued Bauhaus classics, modern Italian plastics manufactured by Kartell and 'Afghan cushions'. The Habitat range includes worthy furniture designs, notably pre-war classics or good modern Italian products. Many of Habitat's in-house designs, however, although ostensibly well designed, are of a disappointing quality, the perhaps inevitable result of being aimed at a wide public.

Two short-lived fads, symptomatic of the youthful search for novelty and lack of concern for durability, were those for paper furniture and for 'blow-up' furniture. A number of designs appeared on the market cut out from sheets of paperboard, easily transported flat and just as easily set up in constructions of a remarkable solidity. Perhaps best-known is Peter Murdoch's child's chair of 1964, designed in England but manufactured in the United States. The team of Scolari, D'Urbino, Lomazzi and De Pas designed the first successful Italian inflatable P.V.C. chair in 1967 for Zanotta Poltrone of Milan. In France, designer Quasar Kahn attracted considerable publicity with his variants on the idea of P.V.C. inflatable furniture.

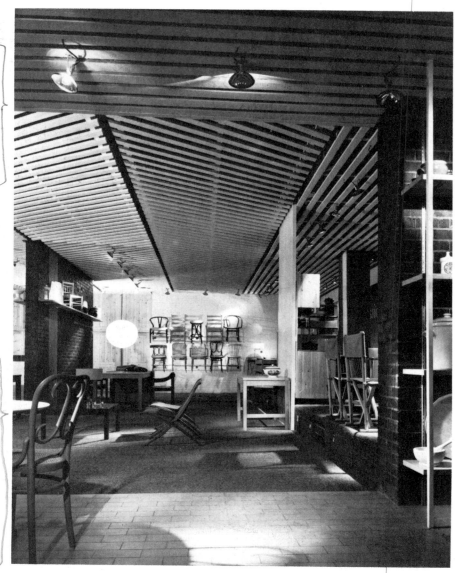

Popular Furniture of the Sixties/Blow-up and knock-down

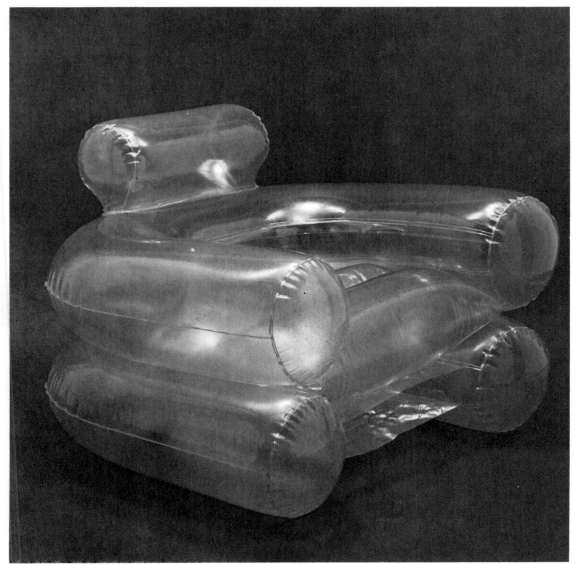

Left Inflatable P.V.C. chair designed in 1967 by the team of Carla Scolari, Donato D'Urbino, Paolo Lomazzi and Jonathan De Pas and manufactured by Zanotta Poltrone of Milan. This design and the numerous imitations which it inspired exploited a rational principle but enjoyed only a brief popularity.

Below left Child's chair in folded paperboard, designed by Peter Murdoch in 1964 and manufactured by the company set up by Murdoch in the United States. This chair has a sturdiness which is surprising in a design which folds into position from a single sheet of laminated paper.

Opposite above Habitat – a shop which has brought about one of the most far-reaching changes of recent decades in the marketing of thoughtfully selected and purpose-designed furniture and goods for domestic use.

Opposite below left and right Habitat furnishings – typical examples of the fresh, inexpensive furnishings offered by this firm which has now spread its influence to a number of countries.

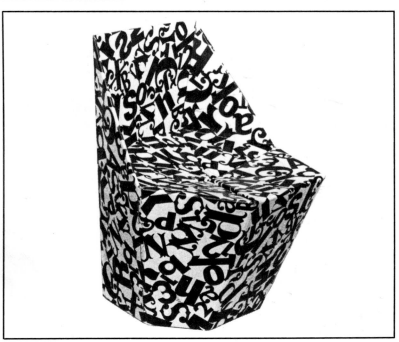

Sixties Pop

An exciting feature of the late sixties emphasis on synthetics was the bold use of bright primary colours. Young taste, in particular, was for splashes of vivid colours, such as the acid colours described in the *Vogue* article already cited. This new attitude to colour was just one facet of the dominant art styles of the decade – Pop Art which sanctified the brash detritus of consumerism, and the Hard Edge Abstract school. Op Art briefly influenced interior design in the mid sixties when a spate of fashionable schemes were published which attempted, with little success, to transform rooms into three-dimensional versions of Bridget Riley's meticulous paintings.

More pervasive was the influence of Vasarely's patterns on carpet or furnishing fabric design. Pop Art had a far stronger influence, both in decorating schemes and in the creation of specific items of furniture. Pop imagery fed the spirit of reaction against the 'good taste' looks of the fifties and early sixties. The Pop mood was carried to its logical conclusion in the furniture and interiors created by a number of artists and decorators who used painterly or sculptural Pop imagery.

The use of areas of bright primary colour on the furniture of this futuristic sixties kitchen suggest the palette of Pop Art. The influence of Pop is also apparent in the use of motifs from everyday life, such as the keys on the storage unit and the figure on the door of the refrigerator – a device recalling the 'Numbers' paintings of Jasper Johns.

Right The colours of the sliding door, chair frames and even of the upholstery closely reflect those of the Pop poster by Lichtenstein: a very direct example of the popularity of fine art inspired design in the late sixties.

Below The lacquered storage units and brightly painted door and screen in this sixties room setting again reflect the colours of Pop Art and also the decade's taste for the impermanent and movable. The eclecticism of much sixties design is highlighted by the presence of the African sculpture.

Sixties Pop/United Kingdom

From London came a host of new designs, simple shapes, seldom in quality materials but bright, young in spirit and timely. Typical was the 'Chair CI' designed in 1964 by John Wright and Jean Schofield, both born in 1940 and trained at London's Royal College of Art, a source of numerous talented designers at that time. The chair, in gloss painted wood of knock-down construction and with bright coloured fabric-covered cushions, was remarked upon in the Whitechapel Gallery exhibition catalogue of 1971 for its 'youthful directness and simplicity.'

Perhaps the best known range of bright-painted plywood knock-down furniture is that designed by Max Clendenning, a designer/decorator who pioneered a bold use of bright colour in interior decoration. Hull Traders produced a chair, the 'Tomotom', which empitomized this same colourful, youthful spirit, the simple cylindrical form in plywood painted in a choice of shiny primary colours.

Several notable Pop furniture designs were created for and available from such shops in London as Anderson Manson, Luckies and the short-lived but remarkable Mr. Freedom. Designing for Mr. Freedom, Jon Weallans, fresh from the Royal College of Art, put his lively Pop ideas into practice and created such nonsenses as a seat in the form of a giant open set of false teeth.

Pop artist Allen Jones won considerable publicity and notoriety for a bizarre range of furniture, which included table, chair and coat stand, each piece modelled in emphatically full relief as a caricatural pin-up girl, clad in fetishistic garb. Three-dimensional versions of the themes constantly explored in his graphic work, Jones's figures are as much sculpture as they are furniture – *objets provocateurs* would be an apt description. Beneath the disquieting and amusing facade of these and other Pop furniture designs is a more serious theme, a theme found in similar measure in the Surrealist furniture of the thirties – a mocking rejection of traditional, preconceived ideas, a questioning of values through iconoclastic humour and surprise.

Above right Bed and pouffes designed by Jon Weallans for Mr. Freedom. This remarkable shop soon established a reputation for lively, often tongue-in-cheek furniture designs. Tommy Roberts, founder of the business, had a shrewd eye for talent and enlisted the aid of young designers, in several instances fresh from the Royal College of Art in London.

Opposite above left 'Chair CI' designed by John Wright and Jean Schofield for Anderson Manson Decorations of London. Painted plywood frame with loose fabric-covered cushions. This chair captured the youthful spirit of London in the mid sixties. It was used in the photographer's studio in Antonioni's *Blow-Up*.

Opposite above right Knock-down chairs designed by Max Clendinning and manufactured by Race Furniture. 'This is the take-it-home-in-a-carton-and-assemble-it-yourself type of furniture which you ought to be able to buy in parts off the shelf like a can of baked beans', wrote one journalist at the time of its appearance.

Opposite Table Sculpture by Allen Jones. One of a limited edition by the artist in 1969.

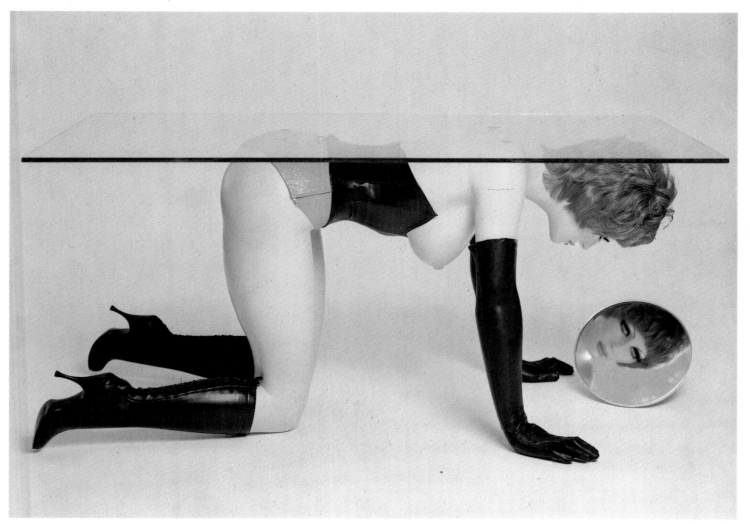

Sixties Pop/France and Italy

Still today as active as ever and one of the most consistently inventive furniture designers to have emerged in the sixties is French artist François Lalanne, a furniture creator too individualistic to be allied with any movement, yet one whose ideas coincided fortuitiously with the 'Pop' spirit. Perhaps best known amongst Lalanne's creations are his sheep seats, at first deceptively realistic as they stand grazing or staring into space. Created in 1965, Lalanne's sheep found their way into some of the most self-consciously fashionable interiors in the world, not least in Yves Saint-Laurent's elegant Paris Left Bank study. Animal themes are Lalanne's stock in trade, used in unusual and often amusing ways. His creations are carefully hand-finished in his country workshops. His is a rare blend of humour and attention to detail. Lalanne's furniture has been exhibited at the Iolas Gallery in New York and in 1975 in Paris.

French Pop artist César has designed some amusing, sometimes alarming furniture, such as his foam seat in which the sitter is invited to settle on a seemingly sharp ridge of upholstery.

In Italy the Pop theme found a lively expression in furniture designs. Some of the most striking examples of Italian Pop furniture were shown in the Museum of Modern Art exhibition, 'Italy: The New Domestic Landscape', held in 1972 under the rather dry sub-title 'Objects selected for their sociocultural implications.' These included a sofa in the form of a giant baseball glove, designed in 1970 by Lomazzi, D'Urbino and De Pas; Gaetano Pesce's 'Moloch' floor lamp of 1970/71, a room-sized version of the anglepoise; a green polyurethane foam mat moulded as giant grass and nicknamed 'Pratone' (large meadow) by the Gruppo Strum, designed in 1970, and Piero Gilardi's set of poly-urethane seats of 1967 which resembled rocks.

The influence of fine art thinking in Italian furniture design found perhaps its most advanced expression in a series of cupboards designed in 1966 by Ettore Sotsass Jnr. and presented as prototypes in the 1972 M.O.M.A. exhibition. Simple rectangular blocks, painted in boldly contrasting stripes of colour in pure Hard Edge Style, these creations were closer to sculpture than to furniture design.

Sheep by François Lalanne in an interior which combines such modern classics as Jacobsen's 'Egg' chair and Saarinen's pedestal table.

Opposite Cupboards designed in 1966 by Ettore Sotsass Jnr. Plastic laminated plywood. These extraordinary cupboards are closer to pure sculpture than to furniture and reflect current trends in post-painterly abstract art. Made up in prototype form for the M.O.M.A. exhibition, 'Italy: the New Domestic Landscape.'

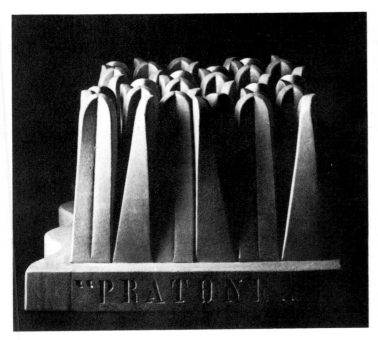

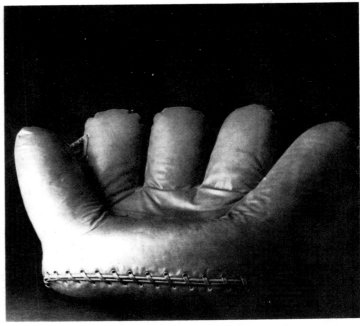

Above left 'Pratone'. Described as a mat, this Pop object in polyurethane was designed in 1970 by the team of Giorgio Ceretti, Piero Derossi and Ricardo Rossi and was manufactured by Gufram.

Above 'Joe Sofa' designed in 1970 by the team of Paolo Lomazzi, Donato D'Urbino and Jonathan De Pas. Moulded polyurethane covered in leather. Manufactured by Poltronova.

Sixties Eclecticism

The years of Pop furniture were also years of nostalgic return to the styles of the turn of the century. Art Nouveau and Edwardian styles enjoyed a popular revival, partly encouraged by exhibitions and new books. Instrumental in commercializing this look was the London store Biba.

Originally a clothes shop, extravagantly and cleverly decorated with a mixture of Art Nouveau-style wallpapers, satins and feathers, Edwardian palm stands and Thonet-style bentwood stands for the clothes, Biba, moving to larger premises, then expanded its retail activity to include the sale of those very same decorating elements which had been so important an ingredient of its own success.

Thonet furniture enjoyed a revival of popularity, Victorian and Edwardian bamboo furniture was enthusiastically bought-up from junk shops and the wallpaper manufacturers Sanderson's and Cole's re-issued Arts and Crafts and Art Nouveau designs, including patterns by Morris and Voysey.

Another aspect of what might be called the escapist styles of the sixties was the international development of a fashionable 'hippie' style of decoration with the object, seemingly, of transforming one's home into a stylish bedouin's tent or harem. It was a style of decoration which tended to make use of available, exotic elements rather than inspire creativity.

The most ubiquitous feature of this mode was the rejection of traditional seat furniture in favour of littered cushions and floor-level day-beds. Giant cushions were a popular and inexpensive spin-off which found their way into many young people's homes as a substitute for chairs and sofas. A rationalized version of this seating idea the 'Sacco' was designed by the team of Gatti, Paolini and Teodoro in 1969 for the Milan firm of Zanotta. The 'Sacco' was a bag of polystyrene granules. Infinitely variable, the design was described by the manufacturers as 'The Chair of 1001 Nights'.

Bentwood enjoyed a revival of popularity in the sixties and the forms first devised by the firm of Thonet were once again the height of fashion.

Right The Biba image of bentwood, palms, dark Art Nouveau wallpapers, satins and feathers provided the inspiration for countless interiors furnished on a budget in the sixties.

Below The 'Sacco' seat, designed by the team of Piero Gatti, Cesare Paolini and Franco Teodoro, 1968–9, and manufactured by Zanotta of Milan. This novel seating idea is a bag of skinflex filled with polystyrene granules which can take any shape.

Italian Supremacy 1

Below right 'Additional System' designed by Joe Colombo in 1968 and manufactured by Sormani. This system was first shown at the Milan Triennale of 1968 and is typical of Colombo's ability to break completely with the traditional concepts of furniture. The system is built up from a series of standard components.

Bottom left 'Chair 4801' designed by Joe Colombo in 1963 and manufactured by Kartell of Milan. Bent and pressed plywood with polyester finish. The chair is constructed of three components which combine to make an attractive interplay of curves.

Bottom right 'Chair 4860', designed by Joe Colombo and manufactured by Kartell, 1965.

Opposite above left Domestic unit capsules designed by Joe Colombo. Colombo was undoubtedly one of the most visionary of the furniture designers of the sixties and part of his vision was to reject the notion of free-standing furniture in favour of all-inclusive capsules.

The most consistently inventive designs in the new synthetic materials came from Italy and ranged in character from stylish sculptural exercises aimed at a sophisticated public to modular furnishings for low-cost mass-production. One of the most inventive designers of the decade was Italian Joe Colombo who set up his own studio in Milan in 1961 and whose early death in 1971 cut short a highly promising career. Colombo devised a remarkable seating range, his 'Additional System', put into production in 1969 by Sormani. First shown at the Milan Triennale, this system allowed a series of six basic units, slices of polyurethane foam, to be combined in various ways to solve different seating problems. A typical product of Colombo's fertile imagination, the range was perhaps too eccentric in appearance to become a commercial success in domestic use.

Colombo's concern was for flexibility in the use of space, achieved by the interchangeability of basic components to provide a variety of potential combinations and serve a variety of functions. He brought an entirely fresh approach to the use of plastics, suggesting many novel applications. In 1969 he designed a series of rooms, presented in prototype by the firm of Bayer A.G. at the *Visiona 69* exhibit within the Cologne International Furniture Fair of that year. These rooms were a vision of a synthetic environment of the future and were intended in Colombo's words '. . . to demonstrate a suggested new way of living . . .'. They were the natural development of a philosophy which had a few years before inspired aggressively new forms first in bright painted pressed and moulded ply and later in plastics. For the Milan firm of Kartell Colombo designed in 1965 his 'Chair 4860', claimed

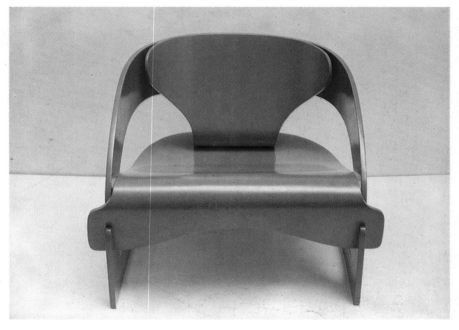

to be the first all-plastic chair to be manufactured by injection moulding.

The firm of Kartell was prominent in the promotion of plastic furniture and put into production the ideas of a number of talented designers. In addition to Joe Colombo, these included Marco Zanuso, Richard Sapper and Anna Castelli Ferrieri. Other Italian firms to make noteworthy incursions into the market with all-plastic furniture included the Milan manufacturers Artemide, with designs by Vico Magistretti and Sergio Mazza, and the firm of C. & B. Italia with an exciting range of designs by Mario Bellini. One of the most sculpturally beautiful designs in plastic to come from Italy in the sixties was the 'Dondolo' rocking chair designed by Cesare Leonardi and Franca Stagi in 1967, a gracious, effortless curve first shown in Milan in 1968.

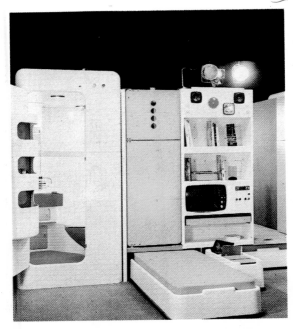

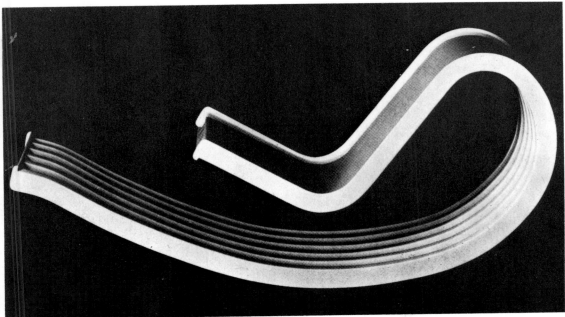

Above Lounge chair designed by Joe Colombo, with fibre-glass shell and hide upholstery – one of the instant classics of the 1960s and completely in keeping with the post-Modernist interior illustrated here.

Left 'Dondolo' rocking chair designed in 1969 by Leonardi and Franca Stagi in ribbed fibre-glass. Manufactured by Elco. A remarkable, sculptural use of fibre-glass in a design of considerable elegance.

Italian Supremacy 2

With the advantage already of over a decade's hindsight, it becomes quite clear that, in addition to lively eye-catching Pop and plastic furniture, a new style of furniture was being developed in Italy in the sixties which has, through the seventies, set new standards of quality and of unassuming but sophisticated style.

Central to the story of this renaissance of a discreetly luxurious approach to furniture design is the Milan firm of Cassina, which has encouraged the creativity of a team of talented designers. Foremost amongst them are Mario Bellini, Vico Magistretti, Afra and Tobia Scarpa. The look which took shape in the sixties and the international spread of which belongs to the seventies, involves quality materials, good woods, marble, a great deal of high-grade hide in designs of a deceptive simplicity, but always with a distinctive flair, a perfection of proportions, a concern for detail and a pleasing tendency to give an impression of solidity and reliability whilst never appearing mundane.

Among the most exciting early designs in this new style must be included a number of luxurious designs for leather-upholstered seat furniture – Tobia Scarpa created his inviting 'Coronado' chair for C. & B. Italia in 1968, his equally luxurious saddle-stitched 'Chair 925' for Cassina in 1965; Mario Bellini created an instant classic with his 'Chair 932' of 1967, an intelligently considered design of interchangeable components belted to-

gether and extendable to form double, treble or longer seating units. Amongst Magistretti's most satisfying designs from the sixties are his 'Chair 892' of 1963, best known in a distinctive red gloss finish, and his 'Caori' table which has been described as a mixture of Italian *brio* and Japanese austerity. These designers and their talented contemporaries have led the way with taste and intelligence out of a confusingly diversified decade and have, in the seventies, consolidated Italy's position as international leader in the field of furniture design.

Right Armchair '892' designed in 1963 by Vico Magistretti and manufactured by Cassina. Available with the beechwood frame in stained, natural or painted finish, the chair is probably best known in a bright red. Straw seat.

Below Low chair designed by Afra and Tobia Scarpa in 1965 and manufactured by Cassina. The chair is available with a frame of ash or walnut and with the foam rubber seat and back covered in hide or fabric.

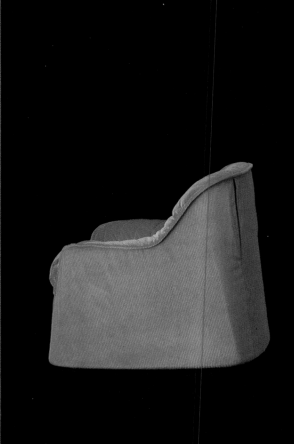

Cassina

Left Room designed by Geoffrey Bennison for the London *Sunday Times* in 1965 to illustrate examples of the best of contemporary Italian design. The scheme includes the 'Bastiano' seating by Tobia Scarpa, the 'Caori' table by Magistretti and the 'Arco' and 'Toio' lamps, both designed by the Castiglioni brothers.

Below 'Ciprea' seating designed by Afra and Tobia Scarpa in 1968 and manufactured by Cassina. Injection-moulded foam polyurethane with a fabric covering.

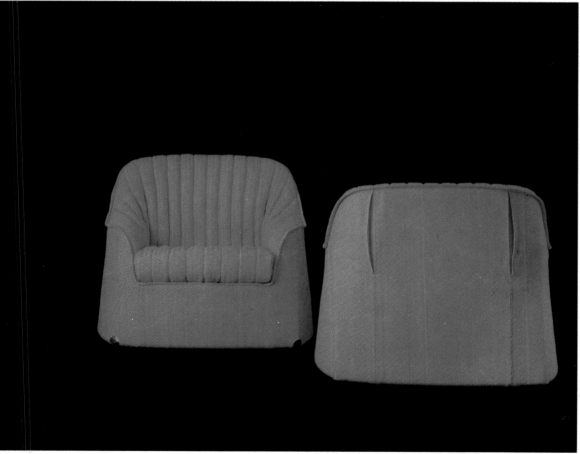

The Seventies/Eighties
Past Craft and Future Technology

The past ten years have witnessed a diversity of trends in furniture design, some seemingly conflicting, which have made of the seventies a decade almost as varied as the sixties. Unlike the sixties, however, a decade which saw the dramatic exploitation of new, synthetic materials in forms which were often without precedent, the seventies saw no real addition to the repertoire of available materials. Changing stylistic concerns have, nonetheless, contributed to the evolution of distinctive seventies looks. Most marked has been the development of the Industrial Style. Better known perhaps by the journalistic catch-phrase 'High-Tech', the Industrial Style seems a more appropriate name, suggesting something more specific both of the style and its long prehistory, from Paxton's Crystal Palace, through Chareau's Maison de Verre to the Centre Pompidou.

In direct contrast to the fashionable emergence of the Industrial Style in furniture design has been the strong revival of the traditions of craft cabinet-making, a revival which started in the sixties and gained considerable momentum in the seventies,

finding talented practitioners in the United States and in British designer-craftsman-teacher John Makepeace. The Scandinavian furniture industries have maintained their long-established reputation for the sensitive compromise between hand craft and mechanized production.

The problems and challenges of furniture design for the contract sector have continued to attract some of the liveliest talents, though the seventies have witnessed few real innovations, rather the increasing sophistication of ideas proposed by the designers and firms who pioneered the concept of contract furnishing.

The most consistently exciting furniture designers of the seventies, however, have surely been the group of Italian designers who emerged in the sixties with their stylish and sophisticated post-Modern Movement ideas. These Italians have created a new image of series production luxury furniture and have also continued to explore a democratic ideal of designing attractive and practical furniture for mass-production at reasonable prices and to high standards.

Architect Michael Hopkins's design for his own home, built in Hampstead, London, in 1975 in pure Industrial Style. The house is constructed of steel framing and decking designed for industrial premises.

Above The Centre Pompidou, Paris, designed by the anglo-italian team of Richard Rogers and Renzo Piano, the most ambitious contemporary application of the Industrial Style in architecture, opened in 1977.

Above Pivoted storage unit designed by John Makepeace and made in his Parnham House workshops, 1978. Constructed in plied birch, the twelve trefoil drawers each have a pastel-coloured acrylic base and are cantilevered from a stainless steel column.

Seventies Contract Furniture

See B overleaf

The contract sector of the furniture industry in the seventies has been dominated by the already well established firms, including notably Herman Miller and Knoll International, while the British firms of Hille and Race Furniture have continued to build on their reputations. Herman Miller's current catalogues are still dominated by the classic designs of Charles Eames; considerable emphasis is placed, however, on the most up-to-date developments of the 'Action Office' range of modular furniture. The publicity explains that 'Years of research into the precise nature and function of the workplace led to the development of the Action Office system. Understanding the intricate problems of people, space, and efficiency takes time. But only with this knowledge can a furniture system be designed to support the people who use it, and meet the ever-changing needs of the organisation.' A significant addition to the Miller seating range was the 'Ergon' chair designed by Bill Stumpf and introduced in 1976, a chair which the firm claimed 'may go further than any other yet produced toward supporting the body in a way that takes anatomical structure into account.'

Knoll, and its British counterpart Form International, like Herman Miller, have relied on the classic designs with which the firm established its reputation, with the addition of a number of fresh designs, including new ideas from the team of Andrew Morrison & Bruce Hannah, Gae Aulenti, Max Pearson and Charles Pollock.

The Italian firm of Cassina has made inroads into the international contract furniture market with its office furnishings marketed under the trade name 'Marcatré'. The basis of the Marcatré range is a highly adaptable system of furnishings designed by leading Italian industrial designer and furniture designer Mario Bellini and known as 'Il Pianeta Ufficio'. Bellini's designs mark 'the transformation of a concept of furniture as a series of objects for equipping a space into the concept of furniture as a fully equipped space system capable of creating office space made-to-measure.' Seating for the Marcatré range includes designs by Giovanni Carini and from the Archizoom Associati studios.

Major contract commissions can allow progressive furniture designers and manufacturers the opportunity to try out new ideas. For the prestigious I.B.M. Centre inaugurated in Helsinki in 1979, the Finnish furniture giant Asko was invited to put into production a new idea for a desk by designer Peter von Knorring. His innovation, known as the '30/60' was a half-hexagon modular unit which became infinitely adaptable in combinations. The modular concept and the ideal of flexibility and adaptability are still the major preoccupations of furniture designers concerned with the work situation.

Right Plan of the 'Action Office' range of modular furniture manufactured by Herman Miller.

Below Plan and arrangement of the 'Molecula' range, manufactured by Race Furniture.

Below right 'Polo' chair designed by Robin Day for Hille, 1979; a typical example of modern contract seating.

EAMES

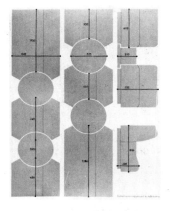

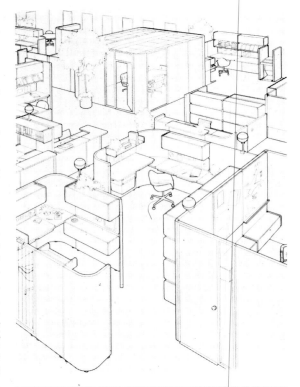

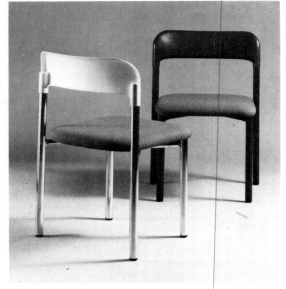

Seventies Contract Furniture

Left Units of the Cassina Marcatré range of office furnishings, designed by Mario Bellini and known as 'Il Pianeta Ufficio'.

Office furniture designed by Peter von Knorring for the I.B.M. Centre in Helsinki, 1979.

Seventies Craft Revival/United States

The ideals of the contract furniture designer, effectively an industrial designer, are far removed from those of the furniture artisan, the craftsman-designer who finds in the creation of finely hand-finished pieces an intimate, even poetic form of expression. A respect for craft and a respect for tradition have long characterized the approach to furniture of the less heavily industrialized Scandinavian countries. In other countries of Europe and in the United States, where the domestic landscape has become dominated by the machine-made, furniture design had, in the eyes of the new generation of craftsmen, become depersonalized.

Craft work has been described as a mediation between the purely practical and the purely artistic. 'Handcraftmanship', wrote Octavio Paz in *In Praise of Hands* of 1974, 'is a sort of fiesta of the object: it transforms the everyday utensil into a sign of participation.' It is a philosophy which has strong echoes of Ruskin and Morris, though today's most prominent furniture craftsmen-designers realistically accept that their clients will be the minority who can afford costly hand work and not the Utopian masses at whom Morris's promises, if not his creations, were aimed. The leaders of the current craft revival in furniture see in the regeneration of traditional skills a means of preserving standards which could all too easily be lost and an opportunity to instill in a new generation of artisans a sense of commitment and a sense of involvement in the creation of their environment, values which are in jeopardy in an increasingly mechanized world.

A respected pioneer of the craft furniture movement is Wharton Esherick, who died in 1970 but whose influence is very much alive. Setting up a hillside retreat near Philadelphia in 1913, he proceeded to carve all the furniture and furnishings which he needed. He has been described as the direct descendant of the Shaker tradition. His was the saying, 'A little of the hand, but the main thing is the heart and the head.'

Probably the most influential figure in American craft furniture today, both as practitioner and teacher, is Wendell Castle, a worthy inheritor of Esherick's mantle. Castle, born in 1932, studied industrial design and sculpture at the University of Kansas, graduating in 1961. Evolving a highly personal style of furniture, he has been the subject of numerous one-man shows and is now represented in major museum collections across the United States. His characteristic approach is to carve out the form of his furniture, usually in swollen and undulating contours, from massive blocks of wood built up in layers. 'My firm', he writes, 'is really quite small, and might most appropriately be characterized as an extension of myself as an artist and designer . . . Everything produced in my workshop is designed, personally supervized and signed by me.'

Another great exponent of the highly sculptural style of American craft furniture is Michael Coffey who, from his workshops in Poultney, Vermont, produces sensual organic forms in rich, polished, often exotic woods, such as walnut, mozambique, rosewood, marnut and cherry. In a 1976 survey of the craft scene, John Makepeace illustrated the work of other Americans whose eccentric sculpted forms evoke the extravagant organic forms of French Art Nouveau, or the baroque Art Nouveau of Gaudí; these included Roy Superior, Peter Danko, Sam Forrest and Stephen Hogbin. Less elaborate, and less costly, is the work of Paul Epp, a craftsman whose straightforward but carefully considered and well-made furniture is designed with price accessibility as an important factor.

Right Mozambique and glass table designed by Michael Coffey and made in his workshops.

Right Games table and chairs in walnut and maple by Wendell Castle, 1977.

Right Desk in English walnut by Wendell Castle, 1977.

Below Ottoman designed and made by Stephen Harris in imbuya wood. The flowing lines and wilfully organic forms of much contemporary American craft furniture calls to mind the forms of certain Art Nouveau designers.

Below Stool designed and made by Paul Epp.

The craft furniture revival in Britain is a recent phenomenon which owes a great deal to the spirit and enterprise of one man, John Makepeace. He had shown an early interest in the craft at a time when it was at its lowest ebb. 'In 1957', he wrote, 'there was very little prospect of becoming a furniture maker. People were giving up such work rather than going in.' He persevered, however, and by 1963 was able to set up his first workshop and exhibition gallery near Banbury in Oxfordshire. Here he developed his highly personal and inventive style and pursued his passion for the craft of wood.

Makepeace's most significant contribution to the furniture craft, however, was his decision to set up a school to train a new young generation of craftsmen-designers in a workshop situation. 'No art school', he maintained, 'was going to produce a woodworker with the sensitivity that wood needs. The only way to work with wood is with total concentration, absolute single-mindedness. It is a material with which you must interact. To determine its form on a drawing board is a very insensitive way to work with it. You have to

become one with it . . .'. Makepeace bought Parnham House, Dorset, in 1976 and in 1977 opened his School for Craftsmen in Wood. The eighties will bear witness to the fruit of his investment in young talent.

The current craft revival has been explained as a salutary escape from urbanism. This same theme emerged in a discussion in 1978 between Bertil Arwidson and pre-eminent Swedish furniture craftsman-designer James Krenov. Krenov's message was described as 'most modern and most urgent. Quite simply it concerns our need for personal things, objects with an inner emotional content in a time of coldness of feelings, mechanization, collectivization, intellectual uniformity, and the casual acceptance of increasing vulgarity . . . What we are discussing now,' added Krenov, 'concerns man's feeling for the quality of life . . . When one tires of impersonal things and an environment that is bad in a variety of ways then we begin to seek certain values of our own. More and more people are doing this, both here in Sweden and, especially, in the U.S.A. and England.' What a contrast to High-Tech!

Chair designed and made by Rupert Williamson in maple and rosewood, 1976. Williamson is amongst the more talented of a new generation of British designer/cabinet-makers.

Chest of drawers designed by John Coleman, a student at London's Royal College of Art, made up in the College workshops and presented by the designer in his graduation exhibit in 1979.

Right Armchair in Macassar ebony and nickel silver, designed by John Makepeace, 1978.

Opposite above Desk with writing surface and legs of buffalo hide, designed by John Makepeace, 1978.

Opposite below left Wardrobe designed by John Makepeace, 1975. The structural frame is of yew with horizontals of Indian rosewood; the vertical panels are clad in buffalo hide. The doors are hinged to fold around the sides.

Opposite below right Hexagonal display cabinet designed by John Makepeace in solid Macassar ebony with spindle-turned glazing bars and incorporating two doors, glass shelves, buffalo hide lining, 1974.

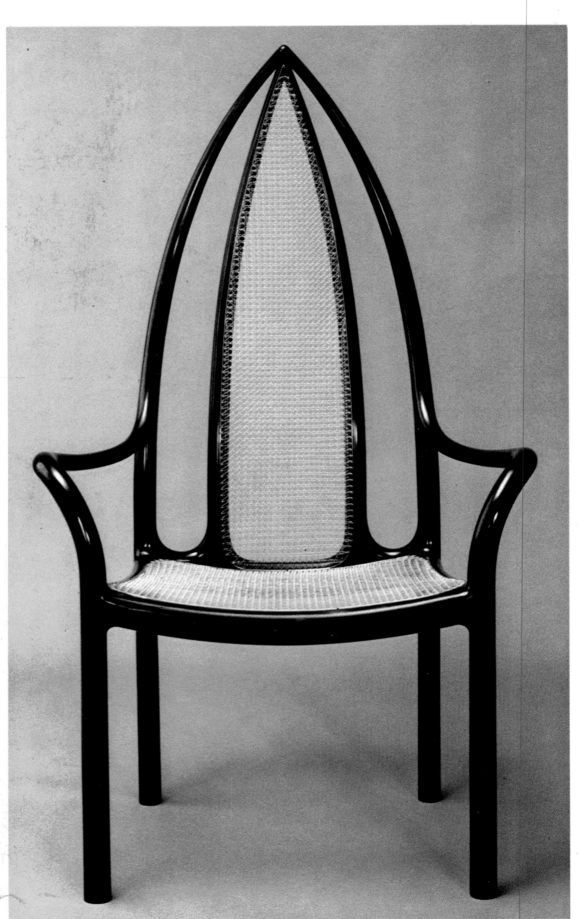

Italian Design in the Seventies 1

The craft ideal, however, as had been demonstrated nearly a century before in the activities of the Arts and Crafts Movement could only ever effectively benefit a minority, could only resolve individual conflicts and not collective design problems. The widest salutary impact on furniture design in the seventies has been that of the contemporary generation of Italian designers, whose increasing contribution was honoured and analyzed by the Museum of Modern Art in 1972 with the major exhibition, 'Italy: the New Domestic Landscape'. The Italian achievement might best be understood in three categories, though the most prominent designs are too versatile, too open-minded to be compartmentalized.

The Italians have made a significant contribution to the environmental concept, though the most visionary of the environmental designers, Joe Colombo, died in 1971 and few of his more advanced ideas were taken beyond the conceptual, prototype stage. They have also created a new style, a new language for luxury furniture, finely made in quality materials, but at the same time conceived for series production. Italian designers have also applied themselves intelligently and with flair to the problems of creating furniture for mass-production at moderate prices.

The 1972 exhibition presented posthumously prototype living units by Colombo outdating the concept of traditional free-standing furniture. He proposed four basic units, kitchen, cupboard, bed and privacy and bathroom. In each, elements folded or pulled out from a movable block and the positioning of these component blocks could be varied according to the primary function of the living space at any given time. Other environmental projects were presented by designers Ettore Sotsass, Gae Aulenti and Alberto Rosselli, projects which still seem as futuristic today as they did in 1972.

More readily appreciated and accepted have been the high-quality furniture designs to emanate from Italy in the last decade. The name of the Milan firm of Cassina has become inseparable from the image of good modern Italian furniture. Spreading its market internationally, Cassina opened a prestigious London showroom in 1980. Marble and hide are favourite materials with the modern Italian school and the mellow attraction of wood is for the most part preferred to metal. Hide has been used to considerable effect for new seat furniture designs during the seventies. Amongst the most remarkable is the 'Cab' range of chairs, designed in 1977 by Mario Bellini. The designer has said of these chairs, in steel and completely covered in saddle-stitched hide, 'they are far more than just supports for the human body or decorative objects, and their concept draws us more deeply to the very roots of our sensibilities.'

Bellini has designed a handsome range of tables for Cassina in the seventies. From 1977 date the 'Colonnato' tables, combining strong modern forms and concepts with that most traditional of Italian materials, travertine or black marble. The tops, in marble or glass, are supported without joints on wide column legs which can be grouped and positioned to suit the individual eye. From the same period date a variety of designs in wood and glass, again using strong, simple forms but with a distinct sense of the sculptural in the design of the sub-structure. The range includes, notably, the 'Corte', 'Basilica' and 'Rotunda' designs.

Vico Magistretti and Tobia and Afra Scarpa, meanwhile, have continued to create imaginative and elegant designs for Cassina. In a luxurious vein, Magistretti has designed two particularly pleasing ranges of hide seat furniture – the 'Maralunga' of 1973 and the 'Fiandra' of 1975. Although a leader in the field, Cassina is by no means the only forward-looking and open-minded manufacturer of luxury furniture. Other firms whose products have attracted international attention and respect include Saporiti, Skipper and B. & B. Under the fitting tribute 'Plus vivant que jamais-le mobilier Italien', French *Vogue* in Dec/Jan 1979/80 presented some of the most interesting designs of recent years. These included designs by Aulenti, Cini Boeri, Giovanni Offredi, Bellini, Magistretti, Enzo Mari, Marco Zanuso, Achille Castiglione, the Scarpas and Angelo Mangiarotti, the latter being shown with one of a series of marble tables for Skipper of bold, architectural design.

The Italian designers have not been completely alone in the use of hide for seat furniture. The Swiss firm of De Sede has grown considerably through the seventies to become one of the leaders in this specialized field of luxury seat furniture.

Right The 'Cab' chair designed by Mario Bellini and manufactured by Cassina. The saddle-stitched hide covering zips into place over the skeletal steel framework. This chair was designed by Bellini in 1977 and is one in a long line of distinguished ideas from this versatile designer.

Above 'Rotonda' table designed by Mario Bellini and manufactured by Cassina.

Left 'Maralunga' hide-covered armchair designed by Vico Magistretti for Cassina in 1973.

Italian Design in the Seventies 2

Below 'Boby' storage trolleys designed in 1968 by Joe Colombo and amongst a number of well-considered designs for plastic furniture to have been launched in the late sixties in Italy and to have enjoyed a lasting popularity through the seventies.

Opposite above right Designs by Gian Carlo Piretti for Anonima Castelli including his masterful folding chair, 'Plia', designed in 1969, his desk, the 'Platone', designed in 1971, and storage shelves. Piretti has produced practical and stylish designs for mass-production at accessible prices.

Opposite above left The 'Pluvium' pivoted umbrella stand designed by Gian Carlo Piretti for Anonima Castelli. The design is manufactured in a range of brightly coloured plastics. The same foldaway principle was used by Piretti in his coat stand, the 'Planta'.

Opposite below left Folding chair from the 'Broomstick' range designed in the late seventies by Vico Magistretti in an endeavour to create a stylish range of furniture designs from standard available components.

Opposite below right 'Plano' folding table designed in 1970 by Gian Carlo Piretti for Anonima Castelli; aluminium and reinforced polyester.

The democratic concerns of many of Italy's leading designers can be evidenced in the continued exploration of plastics and fibre-glass as materials appropriate to the age and lending themselves to mass-production. Several designs introduced in the late sixties have been in continuous production and have not been surpassed for sound good sense and practicality. Amongst these the modular storage units designed by Ferrieri for Kartell, or the 'Boby' designed by Joe Colombo in 1968. Vico Magistretti has produced new ranges of fibre-glass seat and table furniture for Studio Artemide, leaders in the field of synthetics and for whom Emma Gismondi Schweinberger has also created a range of designs.

The firm of Anonima Castelli has made a strong impact on the market in the seventies, and could have done so by virtue of one design alone, the 'Plia' chair, designed in 1969 by Gian Carlo Piretti. This chair, originally in chromium-plated metal and clear perspex, now available in a variety of finishes, has been described as 'a highly complex technological *tour de force* of gem-like visual simplicity. All the previously scattered mechanics have been concentrated in a single cast aluminium hub.'

The same principal has been applied to a tub armchair, the 'Plona Cellidor', and a table, the 'Platone'. All three are inexpensive, highly intelligent designs. Castelli has launched a table, the 'Plana', which folds away with an ease which belies the sophisticated thought behind its design. This table has attracted praise and awards as an instant classic. The 'Planta' plastic coat stand manufactured by Castelli is another clever and elegant example of the fold-away principle which is so

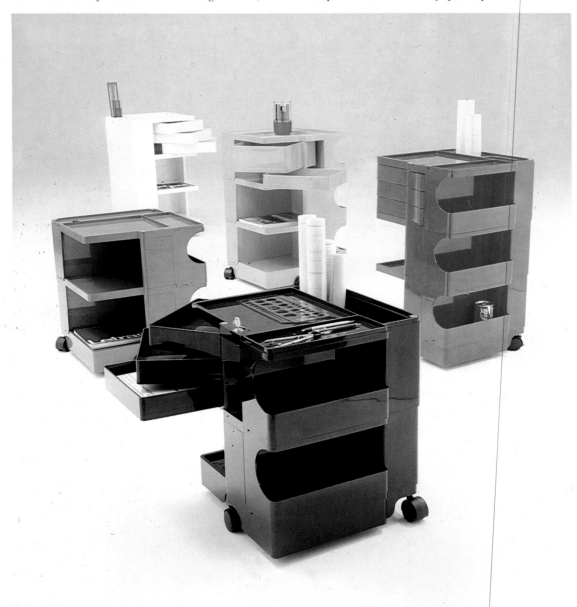

relevant to an age in which domestic space is at such a premium.

Magistretti's 'Broomstick' range of furniture, launched in 1979–80 introduces a return to basic wood elements in furniture with the potential for easy, and inexpensive, series production. In the words of the designer – 'A kind of Robinson Crusoe approach – to make from things that are already available . . . people are bored with plastic.' There are indications that Magistretti is not alone in this approach. Finnish designer Eero Aarnio, whose name was strongly associated in the sixties with fibre-glass, launched a new chair design in May 1969, the 'Avec', a knock-down wood and canvas seat which folds away into a canvas bag. 'Avec is a chair for modern people unwilling to spend much on furniture . . . Avec is for Everyman, the T-shirt of furniture, one might say,' wrote one critic.

Into the Eighties/the Industrial Style 1

The strongest distinctive new style of the seventies, however, has surely been the Industrial Style, an approach to design and decoration which reflects so aptly a state of mind peculiar to the decade, a mixture of cynicism and sophistication which has expressed itself with a harsh realism. A leading interior designer in the style, American Joseph Paul D'Urso, has maintained that 'The best design work in this country is in the industrial sector.' He praises 'products created for transportation and hospitals because of their quality, because the materials are easy to maintain, and because no attempt is made to satisfy anyone's sentimental pre-occupations.' There is nothing sentimental, certainly, about the Industrial Style. It is far more, however, than a pursuit of functional furnishing elements for their own sake; for, indeed, the elements chosen are selected as much for style as for function and the visual language of the Industrial Style is laden with symbolism.

Inevitably, therefore, it has evolved a distinctive vocabulary of stylistic features, each one an expression of the tough image of this new aesthetic. In the area of furniture and furnishings the ingredients comprise both the ready-available and the purpose-designed. The consecration of the Industrial Style came in 1978 with the publication of *High-Tech – the Industrial Style and Source Book for the Home* by Joan Kron and Suzanne Slesin. In their introduction they explained the new fashion for the ready-available industrial design. 'Something is happening in home furnishings: instead of velvet, mover's pads are being used as upholstery; instead of crystal chandeliers, white-enamelled factory dome lights are hanging over dining tables; in place of teak wall units and brass étagères, steel warehouse shelving is holding the books in smart living rooms; and in the bathroom, where gold-plated swans or chrome nuggets once reigned supreme, hospital faucets are adding new cachet.'

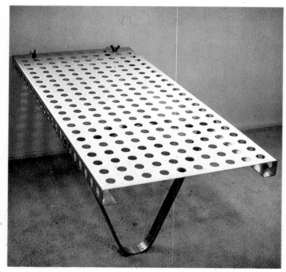

Above Table in perforated sheet metal in the Industrial Style of the late seventies.

Right Interior for 'Joseph' clothes shop in London designed in the late seventies in the Industrial Style. Mies van der Rohe and Le Corbusier furniture fits elegantly into this thoroughly modern scheme in the tough, fashionable style which has found its widest popularity in New York, but of which there are few examples in Europe.

Interior view of the London
Industrial Style home of
architect Michael Hopkins.

Into the Eighties/the Industrial Style 2

A bank of hi-fi equipment prominently displayed in a seventies German interior; the exposure of technical equipment was one characteristic of the growth of the Industrial Style during the late seventies.

Furniture designers and decorators who have espoused the Industrial Style have used an expressive variety of materials in tune with this aesthetic. Metal, not surprisingly, is favoured instead of wood, the connotations of which are far too traditional, and for metal the most modish finish is a sinister and chic matt black. Perforated metal sheeting, polished or painted in bright colours, is another popular material, as is wire-reinforced glass. O.M.K.'s trestle table of 1978 is a classic example of the style, described by the manufacturers as using '... industrial elements to create a sophisticated dining/work table for domestic or contract use.' A recent design by Gae Aulenti in the Industrial Style is her table for Fontana Arte of heavy plate glass with four heavy-duty wheels bolted through on the underside. A wide concertina of black rubber or other materials is another Industrial Style feature which boldly emphasizes flexible construction and has been used *inter alia* in a new chair design from Castelli. The tractor-seat stool is a classic expression of the Industrial Style and variants are manufactured internationally. It is an idea which has its prototype in a sketch by Mies van der Rohe dating from the early forties which serves to emphasize the continuity of thought which, despite changes in fashion and shifts in taste, has characterized the never-ending pursuit of modernity in the evolution of twentieth-century furniture.

Into the Eighties/the Industrial Style 2

Left O.M.K. office designed in 1973 by Rodney Kinsman. The entire system utilizes a simple cast polished aluminium joining knuckle and epoxy coated tubes with perforated steel screen and steel shelves.

Below left Trestle table designed by Rodney Kinsman for O.M.K. in 1978. The drawings are taken from the manufacturer's catalogue and show the trestle element and the wire-reinforced glass top. The matt black epoxy finish to the style framework and the reinforced glass are pure Industrial Style elements.

Below right 'Vertebra' armchair designed by Emilio Ambasz and Gian Carlo Piretti (Open Ark) for Anonima Castelli and launched in 1976. The black concertina column and arms serve a practical purpose in providing the sprung resilience of the chair, but also conform to the Industrial Style aesthetic. Style, as ever, plays as important a role as function.

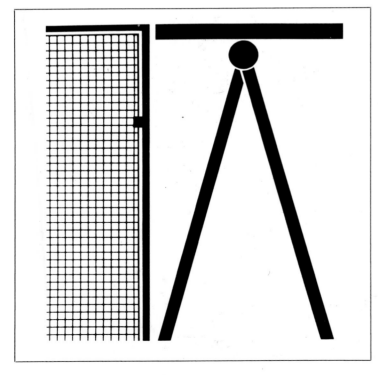

Select Bibliography

AMAYA, Mario: *Art Nouveau*, London and New York, 1966.
ANCIENNE COLLECTION JACQUES DOUCET – Mobilier Art Deco, Provenant du Studio Saint-James à Neuilly, Hotel Drouot Sale Catalogue, 8 November 1972.
ANSCOMBE, Isabelle and Gere, Charlotte: *Arts and Crafts in Britain and America*, London, 1979.
BATTERSBY, Martin: *The Decorative Twenties*, London, 1969.
BATTERSBY, Martin: *The Decorative Thirties*, London, 1971.
BARONI, Daniele: *Rietveld Furniture*, London, 1978.
BAUHAUS, The: Exhibition Catalogue, MIT Press, Boston, 1978.
BAUHAUS, The: Exhibition Catalogue, The Royal Academy, London, 1968.
BEL GEDDES, Norman: *Horizons*, Boston, 1932.
BUSH, Donald J.: *The Streamlined Decade*, New York, 1975.
CASSINA Catalogue, Milan, 1979.
CLARKE, Robert Judson: *The Arts and Crafts Movement in America 1876–1916*, Exhibition Catalogue, Princeton, 1972.
DUNAND, Jean, Goulden, Jean: Exhibition Catalogue, Galerie du Luxembourg, Paris, 1973.
EAMES, Charles, Exhibition Catalogue, Museum of Modern Art, New York, 1973.
FOULK Lewis Collection, The: *Ruhlmann Centenary Exhibition,* Exhibition Catalogue, London 1979.
FOULK Lewis Collection, The: *The Extraordinary Work of Süe et Mare,* Exhibition Catalogue, London 1979.
GARLAND, Madge: *The Indecisive Decade*, London, 1968.
GARNER, Philippe: *Emile Gallé*, London, 1976.
GAUDI, Exhibition Catalogue, Musée des Arts Décoratifs, Paris, 1971.
GUIMARD, Horta, Van de Velde, Exhibition Catalogue, Musée des Arts Décoratifs, Paris, 1971.
HABITAT Catalogues, 1971–1980, London.
HANKS, David A.: *The Decorative Designs of Frank Lloyd Wright,* London, 1979.

HERBST, René: *Pierre Chareau*, Paris, 1954.
HERBST, René: *25 Années U.A.M.*, Paris, 1955.
HOWARTH, Thomas: *Charles Rennie Mackintosh and the Modern Movement*, London, 1952 (new ed. 1977).
JAHRBUCH Des Deutschen Werkbundes, Jena, 1912–1914, Munich, 1915.
JOEL, David: *Furniture Design Set Free*, London, 1973.
JOHNSON, Stewart: *Eileen Gray*, Exhibition Catalogue, London and New York, 1979.
LE CORBUSIER: *Towards a New Architecture*, London, 1927 (Paris, 1923).
MACCARTHY, Fiona: *All Things Bright and Beautiful, Design in Britain 1830 to Today*, London, 1972.
MEADMORE, Clement: *The Modern Chair*, London, 1974.
MIES van der Rohe, Ludwig, Exhibition Catalogue, Museum of Modern Art, New York, 1977.
MUSÉE des Arts Décoratifs: *1925*, Exhibition Catalogue, Paris, 1977.
NAYLOR, Gillian: *The Arts and Crafts Movement*, London, 1971.
PEVSNER, Nikolaus: *Pioneers of Modern Design: From William Morris to Walter Gropius*, London, 1936 (new ed. 1977).
SHAEFER, Herwin: *Nineteenth Century Modern*, New York, 1970.
SCHMUTZLER, Robert: *Art Nouveau*, London, 1964.
SHARP, Dennis, *et al: Pel and Tubular Steel Furniture of the Thirties,* London, 1977.
STUDIO, The, Yearbooks of Decorative Art, London, 1906–30.
THIRTIES: Arts Council Exhibition Catalogue, London, 1979.
TODD, Dorothy and Mortimer, Raymond: *The New Interior Decoration,* London, 1929.
TSCHUDI MADSEN, S.: *Art Nouveau*, translated by R.I. Christopherson, London, 1970.
VOYSEY, C.F.A.: Architect and Designer 1857–1941, Exhibition Catalogue, Brighton Museum & Art Gallery, Brighton, 1978.
WHITECHAPEL Art Gallery: *Modern Chairs 1918–1979,* Exhibition Catalogue, London, 1970.
WINGLER, Hans M.: *The Bauhaus*, Cambridge, Massachusetts, 1969.
YOUNG, Dennis and Barbara: *Furniture in Britain Today*, London, 1964.

Glossary

AMBOYNA – Exotic mid-to-pale coloured wood with a rich natural grain.
ART DECO – Style of decoration which takes its name from the 1925 Paris Exposition des Arts Décoratifs, characterized by fine cabinet-making and the use of luxurious materials.
ART NOUVEAU – Style of decoration which flourished around 1900, especially in France and Belgium, characterized by decoration inspired by organic forms in sinuous curves. Known in Germany as Jugendstil, in Italy as Le Stile Liberty.
BANQUETTE – Bench or wall sofa.
BENTWOOD – Method of steaming and bending wood to form the structure of chairs etc. First developed in the nineteenth century and widely used in the twentieth.
BOISERIE – carved wood panelling or other fitted wooden elements of an interior.
CANTILEVER – Projecting element of a structure which carries an evenly distributed load, the upper half of the thickness subjected to tensile stress, the lower to compressive stress.
CHAISE LONGUE – A chair with an elongated seat.
CYCLE-WELDING – Technique developed by the Chrysler Corporation in 1941 for binding together wood and rubber, glass or metal.
DE STIJL – Name given to a group of Dutch designers from the magazine *De Stijl* published between 1917 and 1931 which advocated a purely formal artistic and decorative style.
DOWEL – Headless pin of wood or metal used to fasten together two pieces of wood by penetrating both.
ÉBÈNE DE MACASSAR – A dark hardwood characterized by a natural streaky marking.
ÉBÉNISTE – Cabinet-maker.
ENSEMBLIER – Designer/decorator responsible for creating every element of an interior.
ÉTAGÈRE – shelf unit.

FAUTEUIL GONDOLE – Tub chair.
GALUCHAT – See Shagreen.
GUÉRIDON – Occasional table.
INLAY – A surface decoration made by insetting differently coloured woods or other materials, such as ivory or horn, as a pattern or representation. Inlay is recessed into the solid wood, unlike marquetry which is a veneer.
LACQUER – A resin drawn from certain oriental trees which is used to create a rich, even, lustrous surface when applied layer upon layer to a wood or metal base.
LAMINATE – Material composed of layers of the same or alternating materials, generally plywood or plywood faced with sheets of plastic.
LIMED OAK – Oak in which the natural open grain pattern is emphasized by rubbing lime into the surface.
MARQUETRY – Decorative veneer in which thin sheets of wood or other materials such as ivory or mother-of-pearl are cut to form a graphic design on the surface of furniture or woodwork.
MEUBLE D'ENCOIGNURE – Piece of furniture designed to fit into a corner.
MODERNISM – Stylistic movement which began around 1900 committed to the ideals of functionalism and rational design and increasingly linked to industrial production.
PALISANDER – Brazilian rosewood.
REPOUSSÉ – Method of making a design in relief in metalwork by hammering from behind so that the decoration projects.
SABOTS – Literally 'clogs', a term used to describe the terminal elements of furniture legs. Often of bronze, although Ruhlmann used ivory.
SHAGREEN – Also known as *galuchat* – the tough, hard skin from sharks, and other fish, generally tinted pale green, pale blue, pink or cream.
VITRINE – Glazed display cabinet.

Index

Page numbers in italics refer to illustrations.

Picture Credits

Robert Adkinson (photo: John Gregory) 41l; Agence Top (photo: J.P. Charbonnier) 180; Albright-Knox Art Gallery, Buffalo, New York, Gift of Darwin R. Martin 57r; Isabelle Anscombe (photo: Richard Holt) 34b, 41t, 79l, 79r, 79b; Artemide (Takis (Furnishings) Ltd., London) 8; Brecht-Einzig Ltd. 185; Brighton, Art Gallery & Museums (photo: Duncan McNeil) 37; Buffalo & Erie County Historical Society, New York 51; Camera Press Ltd. 218; Casa Museo Gaudi, Barcelona 30tl, 30tr, 30bl, 30br; Cassina (photo: Aldo Ballo) 9t, 178t, 200t, 200l, 200r, 205t (Marcatré), 212, 213t, 213b, 215bl; Wendell Castle 207t, 207m; John Coleman 209; Connaissance des Arts 27tr (Musée Horta, Brussels, photo: P. Hinous), 27bl (Musée Horta, Brussels, photo: P. Hinous), 27br (Musée de Beauvais, photo: J. Guillot), 148 (photo: P. Hinous), 176l (photo: R. Guillemot), 177l (photo: R. Guillemot), 177r (architect J. Daladier, photo: P. Hinous), 183t (photo: P. Hinous), 190 (photo: R. Guillemot), 191t (decorator J. C. Maugirard, photo: R. Guillemot), 191b (decorator J. C. Maugirard, photo: R. Guillemot), 194 (photo: R. Guillemot), 199r (photo: R. Guillemot); Robin Day (photo: Mann Bros.) 187b; The Design Council 31tr, 31bl, 31br, 42l, 136, 137t, 137l, 137r, 144l, 144r, 147t, 165, 166l, 168l, 171l, 175b, 197t, 197b, 198l; The Fine Art Society and Haslam & Whiteway Ltd 34t; Fischer Fine Art Ltd., London 65l; The Foulk Lewis Collection, London 72t, 72l, 75b, 76r, 84; Galerie am Graben, Vienna (photo: Elly Niebuhr) 65b, 67b; Philippe Garner 6, 7, 11l, 12t, 13t, 13b, 15, 16t, 17, 18, 19t, 19b, 21, 22l, 23t, 23l, 23r, 24l, 24r, 24b, 25l, 25r, 25b, 26r, 28br, 29bl, 29br, 31tl, 52l, 52r, 54l, 54r, 55t, 55b, 56t, 57l, 60b, 61, 62, 63t, 64t, 64b, 65r, 66r, 68, 69l, 69r, 69b, 70, 71t, 71b, 72r, 73, 74t, 74l, 74r, 75t, 76l, 77, 78, 80t, 80b, 81l, 81r, 82, 83l, 83b, 85, 86, 87, 88r, 88b, 89tl, 90l, 90b, 91b, 99t, 107l, 108t, 108b, 109l, 109b, 110t, 112, 113b, 125t, 125l, 125r, 126b, 127r, 129t, 129l, 129r, 132t, 133l, 134t, 135, 138, 139t, 139l, 139r, 141l, 141r, 141b, 146, 149t, 149l, 149r, 150t, 150l, 150r, 154, 155t, 155l, 155r, 155b, 156, 157t, 157l, 157r, 157b, 159t, 164, 167t, 170, 174, 182, 183b (MGM), 201, 204tr, 206, 207l, 207r; Philippe Garner (photo: Laurent Sully Jaulmes) 88l, 89tr, 89bl, 89br, 90r; The Geffrye Museum, London 35, 36r; John Gregory 120t, 120b; Howard Grey (Musée de L'Ecole de Nancy) 22r; Habitat 9b, 176r, 176r, 188t, 188l, 188r, 196, 214; Hamlyn Picture Library 38r, 49t, 49b, 50, 53b; Hille International Ltd. 152, 153l, 153r, 153b, 158, 159b, 172t, 172b, 179r, 184, 204br; Michael Holford Picture Library 203l; Angelo Hornak 128, 130t, 130b, 131; I.B.M. (photo: Simo Rista) 205b; Interspace 215tl, 215tr, 215br, 219r; The Edward James Foundation 118; John Jesse (photo: John Gregory) 59l, 59r; A. Jones 193b; Jordan Volpe Gallery, New York 44t, 44b, 45t, 45l, 45r, 46l, 47l, 47r; Jan Kaplicky 216l; Keyser, Munich 26t, 26l, 27tl, 28l, 28tr, 29t, 59b, 60t, 63b, 66tl, 66bl, 67t; Ken Kirkwood (Joseph) 216r; Dan Klein Ltd. (photo: John Gregory) 57b; Kodak Museum 43b; John Makepeace 203r, 210, 211t, 211l, 211r (photo: Sam Sawdon); Randell L. Makinson, California 48l, 48r; The Metropolitan Museum of Art, New York 56b (Purchase, Income from Emily C. Chadbourne Bequest, 1972); Musée des Arts Décoratifs, Paris 20; The Museum of Finnish Architecture 12b, 132b, 133r, 133b; The Museum of Modern Art, New York 92, 97, 98, 99b, 100t, 101t, 102t, 102b, 103t, 103b, 104, 105t, 134b, 140, 142l, 142r, 143t, 143b, 145, 147r, 149b, 160, 161, 162, 195l, 195r, 195b, 199l, 199b; The National Trust; Standen, East Grinstead (photo: Academy Editions, London) 39; Osterreichische Nationalbibliothek, Bildarchiv 66t; OMK Design Ltd. 179l, 219t, 219l, Desmond O'Neill Features 193r; The Art Museum, Princeton University 46r (Gift of Roland Rohlfs); M.&J. Pruskin 127t; Race Furniture Ltd. 151l, 151b, 175l, 175r, 179t, 204tl, 204bl; The Royal Academy of Arts, London 43r, 96t, 96l, 96r, 100r, 101b; Sotheby Belgravia 32, 33l, 33r, 38b, 40, 41r, 41b, 43l, 53t, 106, 109, 110l, 110r, 111, 119, 123b, 124, 168r; Sotheby Monaco 114t, 114b, 115t, 115b, 116, 117; Stedelijk Museum, Amsterdam 95t, 95l, 95r; The Victoria & Albert Museum, Crown Copyright 101, 10r, 11t, 11r, 14, 16b, 36t, 36l, 38l, 42tr, 42br, 58, 91t, 113t, 122, 123t (photo: Richard Holt courtesy The Victoria & Albert Museum), 126t, 127l, 173, 189b, 208; Jon Weallans 192; The Whitechapel Art Gallery (Courtesy The Victoria & Albert Museum) 94, 100l, 105b, 147l, 151r, 166r, 167b, 169, 171r, 178 (K. Helmer Petersen, Copenhagen), 179b, 186, 187 (Wilhelm Bofinger), 189t, 193l, 198t, 198r; Elizabeth Whiting & Associates 202, 217; Oscar Woollens Ltd. 107r, 107b.